Dallas CUISINE

Dallas Cuisine

A Sampling of Restaurants & Their Recipes

Compiled and Edited by

DOTTY GRIFFITH

Two Lane Press

First printing August 1993

ISBN 1-878686-06-2

Printed in the United States of America

Cover design, hand lettering, and text ornaments: Calvert Guthrie
Editing and text design: Jane Doyle Guthrie
Food consultant: Judith Fertig

10 9 8 7 6 5 4 3 2 1 93 94 95 96 97

Two Lane Press, Inc.
4245 Walnut Street
Kansas City, MO 64111
(816) 531-3119

To my mother Dorothy, my brother Buz, and my late father Ed, and to Kelly and Caitlin for their love and support.

Contents

Acknowledgments

I extend sincere thanks to all my friends, the chefs and restaurant owners who gladly shared their enticing recipes, and to Prissy Shaffer for her able assistance.

Introduction

Dallas has stayed at the forefront of the Southwestern cuisine movement since it began in the early 1980s. Indeed, Dallas could be seen as the "Third Coast of Cuisine" in the United States. Celebrity chefs Dean Fearing and Stephan Pyles are two of the best known practitioners of this regional cuisine with a national following. Their recipes are represented here as well as those from a number of other well-known restaurants and chefs.

But all in Dallas is not Southwestern. There's plenty of barbecue and Southern-style cooking in the city, reflecting its traditional roots. Tex-Mex is important here, too, as is Cajun and country cooking, a Texas tradition. Diners also find French, continental, Italian, and a number of Asian cuisines in abundance in this city, which is an important convention destination as well as a financial center.

All of our participating chefs and restaurant owners have adapted the recipes for home use. Most of the ingredients called for are easily found in large supermarkets, although a few may require a trip to a gourmet or specialty store or perhaps an ethnic grocery.

This collection of recipes makes a taste of some of Dallas's finest restaurants possible without a reservation. Enjoy the fun of learning and recreating the specialties of your favorite culinary stops.

Dotty Griffith

Beginnings

Vesuvio Salad

3 pounds Roma tomatoes, quartered
1 bunch arugula, coarsely chopped
1 (14-ounce) can hearts of palm, quartered
1 leek, chopped (white part only)
1/2 cup balsamic or wine vinegar
3/4 cup olive oil
Salt and pepper to taste

Toss together tomatoes, arugula, hearts of palm, and leek. Whisk together vinegar, olive oil, salt, and pepper, then pour over tomato mixture. Chill completely (at least 1 hour) and serve.

Serves 8 to 10

MASSIMO DA MILANO
5519 West Lovers Lane
Dallas, Texas 75209
(214) 351-1426
Several locations

Tofu Salad with Tamari Vinaigrette

1 pound tofu
1 stalk celery, finely chopped
1/2 green bell pepper, finely chopped
1/2 red bell pepper, finely chopped
1/2 small red onion, finely chopped

Drain tofu and, using hands, break into small curds. Toss together with vegetables. Pour **Tamari Vinaigrette** over salad and refrigerate for several hours to allow flavors to meld. Serve cold or at room temperature.

Serves 4

Tamari Vinaigrette

2 tablespoons tamari or soy sauce
3 tablespoons bottled vinaigrette
1 tablespoon vegetable soup base (or dried vegetable soup mix)
1 teaspoon Veg-Sal seasoning mix (available in health food stores)

Combine all ingredients in a small jar with a lid and shake vigorously to dissolve ingredients. Refrigerate unused portions.

Makes about 1/2 cup

BLUEBONNET CAFE
Whole Foods Market
2218 Greenville Avenue
Dallas, Texas 75206
(214) 824-1744

Tabbouleh Salad

1 pound bulgur wheat
Hot water
8 tomatoes, seeded and chopped
3 medium cucumbers, peeled, seeded, and chopped
1 small yellow or red onion, finely chopped
2 bunches parsley, finely chopped
1/2 cup mint leaves, finely chopped
1/3 cup olive oil
1/2 cup tamari or soy sauce
1 teaspoon finely chopped garlic
1 teaspoon white pepper
Salt to taste

Place bulgur in a large bowl and pour in enough hot water to cover. Soak for 15 minutes to soften wheat, then drain off excess liquid.

Combine drained bulgur with tomatoes, cucumbers, onions, parsley, and mint; mix well to distribute ingredients evenly. Add olive oil, tamari, garlic, white pepper, and salt. Cover and refrigerate for several hours or overnight.

Serves 8

BLUEBONNET CAFE
Whole Foods Market
2218 Greenville Avenue
Dallas, Texas 75206
(214) 824-1744

Mozzarella and Tomato Salad with Four Dressings

1 pound fresh mozzarella cheese
2 ripe tomatoes
Lettuce leaves

Slice mozzarella and tomatoes uniformly, about 1/4-inch thick. Alternate slices over lettuce leaves on a platter or individual salad plates. Drizzle with choice of dressings and serve.

Serves 4

Classic Italian Dressing

Salt and pepper to taste
Olive oil
Fresh basil leaves, torn into small pieces

Season salad with salt and pepper. Drizzle oil over tomatoes and mozzarella and sprinkle with basil.

Basil Vinaigrette

1/4 cup olive oil
2 tablespoons balsamic vinegar
6–8 basil leaves, plus additional to garnish
Salt and pepper to taste

Combine all ingredients in a food processor and whirl until well combined. Adjust seasoning to taste. Pour over salad and garnish with additional basil leaves.

Makes about 1/2 cup

Oriental Dressing

1 tablespoon sesame oil
3 tablespoons rice wine vinegar
1 teaspoon freshly grated ginger
4–6 mint leaves, plus additional to garnish
1 tablespoon cilantro leaves, plus additional to garnish
Salt and pepper to taste

Combine all ingredients in a food processor and whirl until well combined. Adjust seasoning to taste. Drizzle over salad and garnish with additional mint and cilantro leaves.

Makes about 1/4 cup

Southwestern Dressing

1/4 cup olive oil
2 tablespoons red wine vinegar
1 clove garlic
1 tablespoon cilantro leaves, plus additional to garnish
2 tablespoons chopped canned green chilies, drained
Salt and pepper to taste

Combine all ingredients in a food processor and whirl until pureed. Adjust seasoning to taste. Pour over salad and garnish with additional cilantro leaves.

Makes about 1/2 cup

THE MOZZARELLA COMPANY
2944 Elm Street
Dallas, Texas 75226
(214) 741-4072

Texas Corn Salad

2 (8-ounce) cans whole kernel corn, drained (about 4 cups)
1/2 green bell pepper, seeded and chopped
1/2 cucumber, chopped
1 medium onion, chopped
1 medium tomato, seeded and chopped
1/4 cup chopped pimiento or red bell pepper
1 teaspoon salt
1 teaspoon chili powder
1/2 cup Corn Salad Dressing

Gently combine all ingredients, toss with **Corn Salad Dressing**, and chill for at least 2 hours before serving. (*Note:* Will keep in the refrigerator for 2 days.)

Serves 8

Corn Salad Dressing

1/2 (10-1/2-ounce) can tomato soup
1/4 cup tarragon vinegar
1-1/2 tablespoons prepared mustard
1-1/2 tablespoons Worcestershire sauce
1/2 teaspoon salt
2 tablespoons fresh lemon juice
3/4 cup olive oil
1/2 cup sugar
1-1/2 tablespoons chili sauce
1/2 teaspoon paprika
1/4 teaspoon Tabasco sauce
1 clove garlic, minced

Combine all ingredients in a food processor and whirl until well blended. Store in a covered jar in refrigerator. (*Note:* Works well on a variety of salads.)

Makes about 2 cups

CISCO GRILL
6630 Snider Plaza
Dallas, Texas 75205
(214) 363-9506

Chicken and Spinach Salad with Honey Mustard Dressing

2 pounds boneless, skinless chicken breasts, poached or grilled and cut into bite-sized pieces
1 (10-ounce) bag fresh spinach, rinsed, dried, and stems removed
3 whole carrots, peeled and cut into thin strips
1 red bell pepper, cut into thin strips
1 medium zucchini, thinly sliced
2 tomatoes, cut into wedges

In a large bowl, toss together chicken, spinach, carrots, bell pepper, and zucchini. Chill until serving time.

When ready to serve, toss with **Honey Mustard Dressing** to coat all ingredients, garnish with tomato wedges, and offer to guests immediately.

Serves 4

Honey Mustard Dressing

1 cup mayonnaise
1/2 cup sour cream
1 tablespoon honey
1/2 cup Creole mustard
Salt and pepper to taste

Combine ingredients in a medium bowl and whisk together until well combined. Refrigerate until ready to serve.

Makes 2 cups

CITY MARKET
Trammel Crow Center
2001 Ross Avenue, Suite 200
Dallas, Texas 75201
(214) 979-2690

Grilled Chicken and Roasted Corn Salad with Cilantro Pesto Dressing

4 (6- to 8-ounce) boneless, skinless chicken breasts
2 ears fresh yellow corn, roasted (see note)
Juice of 3 limes
3 cloves garlic, finely chopped
2 jalapeño peppers, seeded and chopped
1/4 cup canola oil
1/2 bunch cilantro leaves, chopped (about 1/2 cup)
Salt to taste
6 (6-inch) corn tortillas, cut into 1/4-by-2-inch strips
1 medium red onion, cut into thin strips
1 medium jícama, peeled and cut into thin strips (about 2 cups)
1 red bell pepper, cut into thin strips
1 green bell pepper, cut into thin strips
1 yellow bell pepper, cut into thin strips
1 Granny Smith apple, peeled, sliced, and cut into thin strips
1 head red leaf lettuce, cleaned
4 tablespoons chopped tomatoes (optional)
4 tablespoons sour cream (optional)

In a small bowl, whisk together juice of 2 limes, garlic, jalapeños, oil, cilantro, and salt. Pour over chicken breasts in a glass dish. Cover and refrigerate for 3 hours or overnight.

Remove chicken from dish and drain excess marinade. Grill breasts over medium-hot coals, preferably mesquite, until cooked through, about 3 to 5 minutes per side. Cut into 1/4-inch strips while warm and reserve.

Fry tortilla strips in hot oil until crisp. Drain on paper towels and reserve.

In a large bowl, combine roasted corn kernels, red onion, jícama, bell peppers, apple, and grilled chicken. Toss with **Cilantro Pesto Dressing.** Season to taste with remaining lime juice and salt. Arrange a bed of red leaf lettuce on 4 serving plates and top with salad mixture. Garnish each serving, if desired, with chopped tomatoes and sour cream.

(*Note:* To roast corn, place ears, with husks, in a 350-degree oven for 20 to 25 minutes. Let cool. Remove husks and silk, cut kernels off cobs, and reserve.)

Serves 4

Cilantro Pesto Dressing

1 bunch cilantro leaves, chopped (about 1 cup)
1/4 cup toasted pumpkin seeds or pine nuts
Juice of 2 limes
3 cloves garlic
1/4 cup grated Romano cheese
1/4 cup olive oil
2 tablespoons mayonnaise
Salt to taste

In a blender or food processor, combine cilantro, pumpkin seeds, lime juice, garlic, and Romano cheese. With motor running, add olive oil in a small, steady stream. Process until mixture is smooth and emulsified. Scrape sides as needed during processing. Fold in mayonnaise and season with salt to taste. Refrigerate until ready to serve.

Makes about 3/4 cup

LANDMARK RESTAURANT
Omni Melrose Hotel
3015 Oak Lawn Avenue
Dallas, Texas 75219
(214) 521-5151

Mesquite Grilled Turkey Piñon Salad

1-1/2 pounds thinly sliced uncooked turkey breast
1/4 cup vegetable oil
1 tablespoon plus 3 teaspoons fresh lime juice
Salt and white pepper to taste
3/4 cup mayonnaise
2 tablespoons Chili Paste
1/4 teaspoon ground cumin
1 teaspoon finely chopped garlic
3 green onions, finely chopped (white and green parts)
1 tablespoon finely chopped fresh Mexican marigold mint, or tarragon
1 red bell pepper
1 poblano chili pepper
1/2 cup seedless red grapes, halved
1/2 cup toasted pine nuts
1 tablespoon finely chopped cilantro
Black pepper to taste
Mixed greens for salad, or bread for sandwiches

Place turkey in a noncorrosive container, such as a glass baking dish or plastic bag. Whisk together oil, 1 tablespoon lime juice, salt, and white pepper. Pour mixture over turkey, coating all sides well. Cover (or seal) and refrigerate for 1 to 2 hours.

In a large ceramic bowl, whisk together mayonnaise, **Chili Paste**, 3 teaspoons lime juice, cumin, garlic, green onions, and mint. Cover and refrigerate.

Over mesquite coals, char the bell pepper and poblano chili pepper until the skins turn dark and blister on all sides. Place peppers in a paper or plastic bag, then close and allow peppers to steam for about 10 minutes. Peel off charred skins and rinse briefly in cool water. Cut off stem top, remove veins and seeds, and cut lengthwise into thin strips.

Remove turkey slices from marinade and reserve liquid. Transfer meat to a well-oiled grill over medium coals, brushing with remaining marinade to prevent sticking, and cook for about 4 minutes per side or until cooked through. Allow to cool, then cut into thin strips.

Toss turkey, pepper strips, grapes, and 1/4 cup pine nuts with mayonnaise mixture. Cover and refrigerate for at least 1 hour to allow flavors to blend. Garnish with remaining pine nuts, cilantro, and fresh ground pepper to taste. Serve mounded over mixed greens or with bread for sandwiches.

Serves 4 to 6

Chili Paste

4 anchos (dried poblano chili peppers)
4 guajillos (dried New Mexican chili peppers)

Cut off stems and slit chilies down the side. Remove seeds and veins. Heat a heavy sauté pan over medium heat and press chilies down flat in pan with a spatula. Sauté for about 3 seconds on each side, just to toast. (Be careful not to burn or chilies will taste bitter.) Remove pan from heat, add water to cover chilies, and soak for about 15 minutes.

Drain chilies, reserving liquid, and transfer to a blender. Process into a smooth, thick paste, adding reserved liquid as needed to blend. (*Note:* Leftover paste may be stored, covered, in the refrigerator for 1 week or frozen in an airtight plastic bag or container.)

BRAZOS
formerly at
2100 Greenville Avenue
Dallas, Texas

Mediterranean Tuna Salad with Sliced Avocado and Papaya

8 (4-ounce) center-cut tuna steaks
1/2 cup finely chopped red onion
1 dried chipotle chili pepper, soaked in warm water to soften, seeded and minced
1 tablespoon minced chives
4 sun-dried tomatoes, soaked in warm water to soften and cut into thin strips
1 clove garlic, minced
1 cup extra-virgin olive oil
6 large basil leaves, torn into 1/2-inch pieces
2 tablespoons fresh lime juice
1 head red leaf lettuce, cleaned
1 ripe avocado, peeled, seeded, and cut into 8 slices
1 ripe papaya, peeled, seeded, and cut into 8 slices

Grill tuna over medium-high heat, approximately 1-1/2 minutes per side. (Do not overcook.) Cool at room temperature until tuna is easy to handle.

Break tuna into chunks and place in a large ceramic or stainless steel bowl. Add onion, chipotle chili, chives, sun-dried tomatoes, garlic, and olive oil. Toss to coat tuna. Leave at room temperature to marinate for 30 minutes.

Add basil leaves and lime juice to tuna mixture. Cover and refrigerate.

Arrange large outer leaves of lettuce on 8 serving plates. Coarsely chop delicate inner leaves and mound in the centers of the plates. Spoon equal amounts of tuna mixture onto each plate, garnish with a slice each of avocado and papaya, and serve.

Serves 8

GALLERY RESTAURANT
Dallas Museum of Art
1717 North Harwood Street
Dallas, Texas 75201
(214) 922-1260

Fresh Mushroom Soup

6 tablespoons butter
1 medium onion, finely chopped
1 pound fresh mushrooms, chopped
3 tablespoons all-purpose flour
4 cups beef stock
Pinch of white pepper
Pinch of nutmeg
1-1/2 cups heavy cream

Melt butter in a large saucepan. Add onion and cook over moderate heat until onion becomes translucent. Add mushrooms and cook for 5 minutes more, stirring occasionally.

Stir in flour and coat vegetables well. Add stock slowly, stirring constantly. Bring mixture to a boil, then reduce heat and simmer for 5 minutes. Add white pepper and nutmeg. Remove from heat, stir in cream, and serve.

Serves 6

THE GRAPE RESTAURANT
2808 Greenville Avenue
Dallas, Texas 75206
(214) 828-1981

Corn and Crab Chowder with Brown Bread Muffins

4 slices apple-smoked bacon, cut into 1/2-inch pieces
1 medium onion, chopped
2 stalks celery, chopped
4 cloves garlic, finely chopped
1 cup dry white wine
1 cup all-purpose flour
3 cups chicken broth
8 new potatoes, rinsed and cut into 1/2-inch pieces
Kernels cut from 4 ears fresh corn (about 2 cups)
1 cup heavy cream
6 ounces crabmeat, cleaned
4 sprigs chervil, chopped
Salt and white pepper to taste

Place bacon in large pot or Dutch oven. Cook over medium-high heat until fat begins to melt. Add onion, celery, and garlic. Sauté for 1 minute, then add wine and simmer until liquid is reduced by half.

Sprinkle flour over vegetables, stirring constantly to eliminate lumps. Gradually add chicken broth, continuing to stir constantly. Bring liquid almost to a boil, then reduce heat and simmer gently for 20 minutes.

Add potatoes and corn to mixture, simmering for 12 to 15 minutes more, or until potatoes are tender. Add cream, crabmeat, and chervil. Cook just until heated through (do not boil). Season to taste with salt and white pepper. Serve with **Brown Bread Muffins.**

Serves 6

Brown Bread Muffins

1/2 cup all-purpose flour
1/2 cup cornmeal
1/2 cup whole wheat flour
3/4 teaspoon salt
1-1/2 teaspoons baking soda
1 egg
1/3 cup molasses
1/3 cup firmly packed brown sugar
1/3 cup vegetable oil
1 cup buttermilk

Preheat oven to 400 degrees. Grease muffin tins and set aside.

In a large bowl, stir together flour, cornmeal, whole wheat flour, salt, and baking soda; set aside. In a separate bowl, combine egg, molasses, brown sugar, vegetable oil, and buttermilk, mixing well. Add wet ingredients to flour mixture, stirring just until combined. Pour into prepared tins and bake for 15 to 20 minutes, or until tops are browned and muffins begin to pull away from the sides.

Makes 18 muffins

LAUREL'S
Sheraton Park Central Hotel
12720 Merit Drive
Dallas, Texas 75251
(214) 851-2021

Spanish Garlic Soup with Lemon Aioli

2 tablespoons olive oil
1 large yellow onion, finely chopped
1/2 cup minced garlic
1/2 cup Roasted Garlic Puree
1 tablespoon dried thyme
1-1/2 teaspoons dried oregano
1/2 teaspoon dried tarragon
3 bay leaves
4 cups rich vegetable or chicken stock
1/4 cup dry white wine
1/4 cup medium-dry or dry sherry
Salt and white pepper to taste
Chopped Italian parsley
Croutons

In a stock pot, heat olive oil until slightly smoking. Add onion, garlic, **Roasted Garlic Puree**, thyme, oregano, tarragon, and bay leaves. Reduce heat and cook until onions are very soft and translucent.

Add stock and bring mixture to a boil. Reduce heat, cover, and simmer for 1 hour. Stir in white wine, sherry, salt, and pepper. Garnish with croutons topped with **Lemon Aioli** and chopped parsley, and serve.

Serves 6

Roasted Garlic Puree

1 cup peeled garlic cloves
2 tablespoons olive oil

Toss garlic cloves with olive oil, wrap loosely in aluminum foil, and roast in a 350-degree oven for 2 hours, or until golden and soft. Allow garlic to cool, then puree in food processor. Refrigerate unused portions.

Makes about 3/4 cup

Lemon Aioli

- 1 heaping tablespoon finely chopped garlic
- 2 egg yolks
- 2 tablespoons fresh lemon juice
- 1/8 teaspoon salt
- 1-1/4 cups olive oil

In a food processor, combine garlic, egg yolks, lemon juice, and salt, and whirl briefly. With motor running, slowly add olive oil and process until mixture takes on a thick, mayonnaise consistency. Refrigerate until ready to serve.

(*Note:* To prepare without using raw eggs, just add specified amounts of flavorings to 1-1/2 cups prepared mayonnaise.)

Makes about 1-1/2 cups

MAIN STREET NEWS
2934 Main Street
Dallas, Texas 75226
(214) 746-2934

Famous Bean Soup

1 pound dry pinto beans
8 slices bacon
1/2 cup vegetable oil
1 cup chopped onions
1 cup chopped green bell pepper
1 cup chopped tomatoes
2 tablespoons chopped cilantro, plus additional sprigs to garnish
1 tablespoon garlic powder
1 teaspoon black or white pepper
1 teaspoon salt

Rinse and clean beans. Place in a large pot and add enough water to cover beans. Soak overnight or bring to a boil, cover, remove from heat, and let sit for 1 hour.

Drain soaked or boiled beans, transfer to a clean pot, and add enough fresh water to cover beans. Bring to a boil, reduce heat, and simmer until beans are tender, about 1-1/2 to 2 hours. Reserve beans and cooking liquid.

Cut bacon into 1-inch pieces and brown in a 3- or 4-quart pot or Dutch oven over medium heat. Add oil, onions, bell pepper, and tomatoes. Simmer until bell pepper becomes soft.

Stir in 6 cups cooked beans. Combine reserved cooking liquid with enough water to make 9 cups of liquid and pour into pot with beans and vegetables. Stir in cilantro, garlic powder, pepper, and salt. Bring to a boil, lower heat, and simmer about 15 minutes. Mash some of the beans with the back of a spoon to thicken soup. Adjust seasoning to taste.

Ladle into bowls, garnish each with a sprig of fresh cilantro, and serve. (*Note:* May be made up to 2 hours ahead.)

Serves 12

MIA'S TEX-MEX RESTAURANT
4322 Lemmon Avenue
Dallas, Texas 75219
(214) 526-1020

Tortilla Soup

7 (6-inch) corn tortillas
3 tablespoons corn oil, plus additional
6 cloves garlic, chopped
1 tablespoon chopped epazote or cilantro
1-1/2 pounds onions, peeled and pureed
3-1/2 pounds tomatoes, peeled, seeded, and pureed
1 tablespoon ground cumin
6 guajillos (dried New Mexican chili peppers), seeded
2 bay leaves
1/4 cup tomato paste
8 cups chicken stock
Salt and cayenne pepper to taste
1 cooked chicken breast, cut into strips
1 avocado, peeled, seeded, and cubed
1 cup shredded cheddar cheese

Coarsely chop 4 tortillas. Cut remaining 3 tortillas into thin strips and reserve. Heat oil in a large pot over medium heat. Fry chopped tortillas and garlic until garlic turns light brown and tortillas become crisp. Add epazote, onion puree, and tomato puree. Bring liquid to a boil, then add cumin, chilies, bay leaves, tomato paste, and chicken stock. Bring to a boil again, then reduce heat and simmer, stirring frequently, for 30 minutes.

Fry remaining tortillas strips in a small amount of oil until crisp. Drain on absorbent paper and reserve.

Skim any fat from surface of soup. Strain and season with salt and cayenne pepper. Pour into warm bowls and garnish each with an equal portion of chicken breast strips, avocado cubes, shredded cheese, and crisp tortilla strips. Serve immediately.

Serves 8

THE MANSION ON TURTLE CREEK
2821 Turtle Creek Boulevard
Dallas, Texas 75219
(214) 559-2100

Sopa de Fideo

8 cups chicken broth
6 bay leaves
1 whole boneless, skinless chicken breast
1 teaspoon olive oil
1 poblano chili pepper, seeded and cut into thin strips
1 small yellow onion, sliced
1 tablespoon coarsely chopped garlic
3 medium tomatoes
8 ounces dry vermicelli, broken into 3-inch pieces
1/4 cup warm water
1 guajillo (dried New Mexican chili pepper)
6–8 cilantro sprigs, leaves removed and reserved
1/2 teaspoon ground thyme
1/2 teaspoon ground cumin
1/2 teaspoon ground marjoram
1 tablespoon tomato paste

In a large saucepan, combine chicken broth, bay leaves, and chicken breast. Bring liquid to a boil, reduce heat, and simmer for 15 to 20 minutes, or until chicken is cooked. Remove bay leaves and discard. Remove chicken, cool, and chop; reserve. Keep broth warm over very low heat.

Heat olive oil in a small saucepan. Add poblano pepper strips, half the sliced onion, and garlic. Sauté until vegetables are soft, about 5 minutes. Remove from pan and reserve for use as garnish.

Place remaining onion in the same pan and sauté until soft. Set aside.

Place whole tomatoes into hot chicken broth for 1 minute or until skins pop. Remove tomatoes and slip off skins. Set tomatoes aside.

Add vermicelli to simmering broth and cook for 4 to 6 minutes or until al dente. Remove pasta from broth and reserve.

Pour warm water over dried chili pepper to soften for 10 minutes. Chop cilantro stems and add to broth along with thyme, cumin, marjoram, and tomato paste. Simmer for 10 minutes.

Drain softened chili pepper, remove stem, and slit to scrape out seeds. Place seeded chili pepper, peeled tomatoes, and sautéed onion in a blender or food processor and whirl to a paste. Add to broth along with pasta and chopped chicken. Chop cilantro leaves to make about 2 tablespoons, then use to garnish soup along with reserved poblano pepper strips and cooked onion slices.

Serves 8

CHIQUITA MEXICAN CUISINE
4514 Travis Street, Suite 105
Dallas, Texas 75205
(214) 521-0092

Fried Parsley

2 bunches fresh parsley
Vegetable oil for deep-frying
Juice of 1/2 lemon
1 lemon, cut into wedges
Salt

Thoroughly rinse parsley, keeping florets together in a bunch. Shake vigorously to remove excess water, then wrap in damp paper towels and refrigerate until ready to use.

Heat oil in a deep-fryer to 375 degrees. Grasp stems of parsley bunch firmly and twist so that stems break off cleanly, just below florets. Place florets in deep-fryer basket and briefly dip in hot oil, about 5 seconds. Parsley should not brown, but remain a deep green color.

Shake out excess oil, then quickly drain parsley on paper towels. Sprinkle lightly with salt and lemon juice. Garnish with lemon wedges and serve.

Serves 4

EWALD'S CONTINENTAL RESTAURANT
Stoneleigh Hotel
2927 Maple Avenue
Dallas, Texas 75201
(214) 871-2523

Warm Crab Dip in New Potato Cups

12 small new potatoes
1 cup crabmeat, cleaned
2 tablespoons dry white wine
4 ounces cream cheese, softened
1 tablespoon fresh lemon juice
1 clove garlic, finely chopped
2 tablespoons finely chopped chives
1/2 teaspoon Worcestershire sauce
Dash of Tabasco sauce
Salt and pepper to taste
1 teaspoon paprika

Place potatoes in a saucepan and add enough water to cover. Bring to a boil and cook until potatoes can be pierced easily with a fork, about 15 to 20 minutes. Drain potatoes and allow to cool enough to handle.

Cut potatoes in half and scoop out some of the center of each, leaving a substantial shell for stuffing. Place potatoes on a baking sheet and set aside.

In a food processor, combine crabmeat, wine, cream cheese, lemon juice, garlic, chives, Worcestershire and Tabasco sauces, salt, and pepper. Process to blend well and evenly mix ingredients. Fill potatoes with crab mixture and sprinkle each with a small amount of paprika. Bake in a 350-degree oven for 6 to 8 minutes or until heated through. Serve warm.

Serves 6

THE FRENCH ROOM
The Adolphus Hotel
1321 Commerce Street
Dallas, Texas 75202
(214) 742-8200

Spicy Shrimp Dip

2 pounds peeled, deveined shrimp, boiled and cooled
1 (8-ounce) package cream cheese, softened
1/2 cup mayonnaise
1 cup Brockles Special Dressing (available in better groceries, or may substitute Thousand Island dressing)
1/4 cup minced green onions (white and green parts)
1 small onion, grated
4 teaspoons Tabasco sauce
1 tablespoon seasoned salt
1 tablespoon freshly grated horseradish
Assorted crackers

Finely chop shrimp and set aside.

Blend cream cheese with mayonnaise and dressing. Stir in shrimp, onions, Tabasco sauce, seasoned salt, and horseradish. Adjust seasoning to taste. Serve on crackers. (*Note:* Recipe may be halved and/or refrigerated overnight.)

Makes about 6 cups

S&D OYSTER COMPANY
2701 McKinney Avenue
Dallas, Texas 75204
(214) 880-0111

Pesto Bread with Sun-Dried Tomato Butter

1 loaf French bread
1/2 cup Pesto
3/4 cup grated Parmesan cheese

Halve the loaf lengthwise. Spread equal amounts of **Sun-Dried Tomato Butter** and **Pesto** on the cut side of each half, followed by an even sprinkling of Parmesan cheese. Bake at 400 degrees until hot and cheese is lightly browned, about 10 minutes.

Serves 6

Sun-Dried Tomato Butter

3/4 cup (1-1/2 sticks) butter, softened slightly
2 ounces (about 1/4 cup) sun-dried tomatoes
1 tablespoon chopped parsley
1 ounce chopped chives
1 green onion, chopped (white part only)

Soak sun-dried tomatoes in hot water for about 15 minutes to soften, then drain and coarsely chop. Combine with butter, parsley, chives, and green onion in a food processor. Whirl until ingredients are blended and butter is smooth. Chill to set before serving.

Makes about 3/4 cup

Pesto

1 cup basil leaves
2–4 cloves garlic
1/2 cup grated Parmesan cheese
Salt and pepper to taste
1 cup olive oil

Whirl basil, garlic, and Parmesan cheese in a food processor until all ingredients are finely chopped. With motor running, slowly add olive oil and process until mixture becomes smooth. Refrigerate unused portions.

Makes about 1 cup

DEEP ELLUM CAFE
400 2706 Elm Street
Dallas, Texas 75226
(214) 741-9012

Focaccia Pugliese

1 pound potatoes (about 3 medium), peeled
1 package yeast
1/2 cup warm water (about 110 degrees)
4 cups unbleached all-purpose flour
1 tablespoon olive oil, plus additional
1 teaspoon salt
1 large or 2 medium tomatoes, thinly sliced
1/2 cup sliced black olives
1 small onion, thinly sliced
2 tablespoons fresh oregano or 1 tablespoon dried

Place potatoes in a large pot with enough water to cover. Bring to a boil and simmer until potatoes are tender enough to pierce easily with a fork. Drain potatoes, cut into cubes, and mash in a large bowl.

Dissolve yeast in warm water. Stir with a fork and set aside.

Add flour to mashed potatoes along with 1 tablespoon olive oil and salt. Add yeast, mixing well. Knead until dough is shiny and elastic.

Lightly grease a large clean bowl with olive oil and transfer dough to it. Cover bowl with a layer of plastic wrap and a tea towel, then set in a warm place. Let dough rise for about 1 hour or until doubled in bulk.

Preheat oven to 400 degrees. Lightly grease 2 pizza or jelly-roll pans with olive oil. Divide dough and press into pans, all the way to the edges. Using your thumb, make indentions in the dough. Arrange sliced tomatoes, olives, onions, and oregano over each piece of dough (use more or less as desired). Drizzle each with olive oil and bake for about 30 minutes, or until edges are golden.

Serves 12

RISTORANTE SAVINO
2929 North Henderson
Dallas, Texas 75206
(214) 826-7804

Ricotta and Goat Cheese Crêpes with Tomato Sauce

2 tablespoons clarified butter (see note), melted, plus additional for pan (may substitute vegetable oil)
1 cup all-purpose flour, sifted
2 eggs
1 cup milk
Pinch each of salt and nutmeg
1-1/2 pounds ricotta cheese
14 ounces herbed goat cheese
2 eggs, beaten
1/4 teaspoon pepper, or to taste
1/4 cup grated Montasio or Parmesan cheese

Combine clarified butter, flour, eggs, milk, salt, and nutmeg in a food processor and whirl until smooth. Refrigerate batter for 1 hour.

Preheat a crêpe pan or small sauté pan and brush with additional melted butter. Pour about 1/4 cup batter into hot pan and quickly tilt pan to spread batter evenly. Turn crêpes after 30 seconds and cook on reverse side for about 15 seconds. Remove from pan and stack on a plate. Repeat using remaining batter. (Makes about ten 8-inch crêpes.) Cover crêpes with a towel to keep moist.

Combine ricotta and goat cheeses. Add beaten eggs and season to taste with salt and pepper. Divide mixture among crêpes and spread evenly over each. Roll crêpes and set aside, seam-side down. Grease an oblong baking dish. Cut each rolled crêpe into thirds. Stand pieces of crêpes on end, sides touching, in baking dish and sprinkle with Montasio or Parmesan cheese. Bake at 350 degrees for 30 to 45 minutes. Spoon a small amount of **Tomato Sauce** over the crêpes as they are served.

(*Note:* To clarify butter, melt in a heavy saucepan over low heat. Skim froth from surface, then carefully pour clear yellow liquid into another dish, leaving milky residue in pan.)

Serves 8

Tomato Sauce

1 clove garlic, finely chopped
2 tablespoons extra-virgin olive oil
2 cups chopped tomatoes, peeled and seeded
Salt and pepper to taste
10 basil leaves, cut into thin strips

Place garlic and olive oil in a small saucepan. Cook over moderate heat until garlic releases its aroma. Stir in tomatoes and simmer for about 5 minutes. Add salt and pepper, then stir in basil. Serve at room temperature.

Makes about 1-1/2 cups

THE MOZZARELLA COMPANY
2944 Elm Street
Dallas, Texas 75226
(214) 741-4072

Chicken Bombay Sandwiches

2 cups cooked and slivered chicken breasts
1/2 cup chopped, crisply cooked bacon
1/4 cup grated white cheddar cheese
1/4 cup chopped red bell pepper
2 tablespoons finely chopped green onions (white part only)
1 teaspoon finely chopped garlic
Up to 1-1/2 cups mayonnaise
Dash of Tabasco sauce, or to taste
1-1/2 tablespoons high-quality curry powder
1/2 teaspoon turmeric
Salt and pepper to taste
10 slices raisin bread, toasted
Small bunches of grapes

In a bowl, combine chicken, bacon, cheese, bell pepper, green onion, and garlic. Toss to combine. Add just enough mayonnaise to bind ingredients, along with Tabasco sauce, curry powder, turmeric, salt, and pepper. Stir well to incorporate ingredients. Spread evenly onto raisin bread and cut slices in half. Place halves together and arrange on a serving platter. Garnish with bunches of grapes and serve.

Serves 4 to 6

LADY PRIMROSE'S THATCHED COTTAGE PANTRY
The Crescent
2200 Cedar Springs Road
Dallas, Texas 75201
(214) 871-8334

Broiled Quail with Pancetta and Mustard

8 quail, cleaned and trimmed
1/2 cup stone-ground mustard
1/2 teaspoon cracked pepper
2 tablespoons grappa or brandy
1 tablespoon olive oil, plus additional for basting
8 slices pancetta (Italian bacon)
Cooked pasta or mixed greens (optional)

Cut each quail down the back on both sides of the backbone. Cut away neck and backbone. Spread each bird open, skin-side up, on a work surface. Press each firmly to flatten, then set aside.

In a small bowl, stir together mustard and pepper. Gradually blend in grappa, then olive oil. Brush inside of each quail with 1 teaspoon of mustard mixture. Top with a slice of pancetta and fasten with a toothpick.

Lightly brush underside of quail with additional olive oil. Place under a preheated broiler for 4 minutes. Turn and brush skin side with mustard mixture. Broil for 2 to 3 minutes longer, or until skin begins to brown. If desired, serve on a bed of cooked pasta or mixed greens.

Serves 8

ACTUELLE
500 Crescent Court, Suite 165
Dallas, Texas 75201
(214) 855-0440

Gulf Crab Cakes with Lemon-Pepper Mayonnaise and Grilled Romaine Salad

- 2 pounds lump crabmeat, cleaned
- 1 red bell pepper, finely chopped
- 1 yellow bell pepper, finely chopped
- 1 green bell pepper, finely chopped
- 1/2 red onion, very finely chopped
- 1/2 jalapeño pepper, seeded and finely chopped
- 8 sprigs cilantro, chopped
- 3 eggs, beaten
- 1-1/3 cups dry bread crumbs
- 2 teaspoons salt
- 1 teaspoon fresh lime juice
- 2 tablespoons canola or other light oil

Place crabmeat in a large bowl. Add bell peppers, onion, jalapeño pepper, cilantro, eggs, bread crumbs, salt, and lime juice. Mix very gently to avoid breaking up lumps of crabmeat. Mixture should just adhere to form cakes. Divide into 12 portions and flatten slightly to form plump cakes.

Heat oil in a medium sauté pan over medium-high heat. Carefully place crab cakes in pan and sauté until golden and cooked through. When done, remove from pan and drain. Keep warm.

Place about 1/4 cup **Grilled Romaine Salad** in the centers of 4 serving plates and top with **Garlic Croutons.** Arrange 3 crab cakes around the salad and top each with a teaspoon of **Lemon-Pepper Mayonnaise.** Serve immediately.

Serves 4

Grilled Romaine Salad

- 1 head romaine lettuce, rinsed and dried (leave whole)
- 1 head radicchio, rinsed and dried (leave whole)
- 2 tablespoons olive oil
- 2 tablespoons balsamic vinegar
- Salt and pepper to taste

Prepare medium coals. Split heads of romaine and radicchio lengthwise. Using 1 tablespoon each of oil and vinegar, lightly brush split surface of lettuces, then season with salt and pepper. Grill, split-surface down, for 30 seconds. Lettuce should wilt only slightly. Turn and grill other sides for 15 seconds more. Remove from heat and chill. Cut into thin strips across stem line at 1/2-inch intervals. To serve, toss lettuce strips with remaining 1 tablespoon each of olive oil and balsamic vinegar. Season with salt and pepper.

Serves 4

Garlic Croutons

1 loaf French bread
1/4 cup olive oil
2 garlic cloves, halved

Preheat oven to 325 degrees. Cut loaf diagonally into oval slices about 1/4-inch thick. Rub both sides of slices with cut surface of garlic cloves. Brush lightly with oil and bake for 10 to 15 minutes, until crisp and golden. Store unused portions in an airtight bag or container.

Makes several dozen croutons

Lemon-Pepper Mayonnaise

2 egg yolks
1 anchovy fillet, mashed
1 clove garlic, finely chopped
1 teaspoon Dijon mustard
3/4 teaspoon white wine vinegar
1/2 teaspoon finely grated lemon zest
1 cup light olive oil
2 teaspoons fresh lemon juice
Salt to taste
1 teaspoon cracked pepper
2 teaspoons finely grated Romano cheese

In a large mixing bowl, combine egg yolks, anchovy, garlic, mustard, vinegar, and lemon zest. Whisk together until mixture becomes thick and light in color. Whisk in oil a few drops at a time, then increase amount of each addition up to a tablespoon. (Completely incorporate each addition before adding more oil.) When all oil has been used, add lemon juice, salt, pepper, and Romano cheese. Adjust seasoning to taste. Refrigerate until ready to serve.

(*Note:* To prepare without using raw eggs, just add specified amounts of flavorings to 1-1/4 cups prepared mayonnaise.)

Makes about 1-1/2 cups

THE CONSERVATORY
Hotel Crescent Court
400 Crescent Court
Dallas, Texas 75201
(214) 871-3242

Shrimp Pacific

1 pound medium shrimp, peeled and deveined
3 tablespoons unsalted butter
4 shallots, finely chopped
4 broccoli florets, steamed
8 mushrooms, sliced
1/2 zucchini, peeled and cut into thin strips
1 teaspoon Spices Seascape
1/2 cup dry white wine
2 cups heavy cream
1/4 cup chopped parsley
Salt to taste

Rinse and pat dry shrimp. In a heavy skillet, melt 1-1/2 tablespoons butter. Add shrimp, shallots, broccoli, mushrooms, zucchini, and **Spices Seascape.** Sauté over medium-high heat for 1 minute. Add white wine and stir to scrape up any bits that may stick to the pan. Stir in cream.

When shrimp turn pink, after 2 to 3 minutes cooking time, remove from pan and set aside. Continue simmering until cream mixture is reduced by half. Add remaining 1-1/2 tablespoons butter in small pieces, stirring constantly. Add parsley and adjust seasoning to taste. Spoon warm sauce over shrimp and serve.

Serves 4

Spices Seascape

1 tablespoon ground cumin
1-1/2 teaspoons cayenne pepper
1 tablespoon gumbo filé powder
1 tablespoon paprika
3/4 teaspoon celery salt
1 tablespoon dried sage
1-1/2 teaspoons nutmeg
1-1/2 teaspoons saffron
1-1/2 teaspoons curry powder
1 tablespoon coriander

Combine all ingredients in an airtight container. Use to season seafood.

Makes 3/4 cup

CAFE PACIFIC
24 Highland Park Village
Dallas, Texas 75205
(214) 526-1170

Lobster-Papaya Quesadillas with Pineapple-Serrano Salsa

- 12 (6-inch) flour tortillas
- 12 ounces Monterey Jack cheese, shredded
- 6 ounces lobster meat, diced
- 1 large (1/2-pound) papaya, peeled, seeded, and diced
- 2 tablespoons chopped cilantro
- 2 teaspoons minced jalapeño pepper
- 2 tablespoons vegetable oil

Lay out 6 tortillas and sprinkle each with cheese, lobster, papaya, cilantro, and jalapeño pepper. Top each with another tortilla.

Heat oil in large skillet over medium heat. In batches, brown quesadillas on both sides (as for a grilled cheese sandwich), adding additional oil if necessary. Keep warm. Using a very sharp knife or pizza wheel, cut each quesadilla into 4 to 6 wedges. Serve warm with **Pineapple-Serrano Salsa.**

Serves 6

Pineapple-Serrano Salsa

- 2 cups finely chopped fresh pineapple
- 1 cup seeded and diced tomato
- 3/4 cup diced red onion
- 2 teaspoons seeded and minced serrano chili pepper
- 3 tablespoons chopped cilantro
- 1 teaspoon minced garlic
- 2 tablespoons olive oil
- 2 tablespoons fresh lime juice
- 1-1/2 teaspoons pepper
- 2 teaspoons salt

Combine all ingredients except salt. Stir in salt just before serving.

Makes 4-1/2 cups

DAKOTA'S
600 North Akard Street
Dallas, Texas 75201
(214) 740-4001

Warm Lobster Tacos with Yellow Tomato Salsa and Jícama Salad

4 (1-pound) lobsters
6 (8-inch) flour tortillas
3 tablespoons corn oil
1 cup grated jalapeño Jack cheese
1 cup shredded fresh spinach

Preheat oven to 300 degrees. Fill a large stock pot with lightly salted water and bring to a boil over high heat. Add lobsters and cook for about 8 minutes or just until done. Drain and let lobsters cool slightly.

Wrap tortillas tightly in foil and place in preheated oven for about 15 minutes or until heated through. Keep warm until ready to use.

Remove meat from lobster tails, being careful not to tear into pieces. Slice meat into thin medallions or coarsely chop if meat breaks apart. (*Note:* Can refrigerate up to 1 day if preparing lobster in advance.)

Heat oil in a medium sauté pan over medium heat and sauté lobster medallions just until heated through. Spoon equal portions of warm lobster medallions into the center of each warm tortilla. Sprinkle with equal portions of grated cheese and shredded spinach. Roll tortillas into cylinders and place each on a warm serving plate. Surround tacos with **Yellow Tomato Salsa** and garnish with a small mound of **Jícama Salad** on each side.

Serves 6

Yellow Tomato Salsa

2 pints yellow cherry tomatoes or 1 pound yellow tomatoes
1 large shallot, very finely chopped
1 large clove garlic, very finely chopped
2 tablespoons finely minced cilantro
1 tablespoon champagne vinegar or white wine vinegar
2 serrano chili peppers, seeded and finely chopped
2 teaspoons fresh lime juice
Salt to taste
1 tablespoon maple syrup (use only if tomatoes are not sweet enough)

In a food processor, pulse tomatoes until well chopped. (Do not puree.) Transfer tomatoes and their juices to a mixing bowl and stir in shallot, garlic, cilantro, vinegar, chilies, lime juice, and salt, mixing well. Add maple syrup, if needed, to balance flavor and sweeten slightly. Cover and refrigerate for at least 2 hours or until very cold. (*Note:* May be refrigerated up to 8 hours before serving.) Adjust seasoning to taste.

Makes about 3 cups

Jícama Salad

1/2 small jícama, peeled and cut into thin strips
1/2 small red bell pepper, cut into thin strips
1/2 small yellow bell pepper, cut into thin strips
1/2 small zucchini, halved lengthwise, seeded, and sliced thinly
1/2 small carrot, peeled and cut into thin strips
4 tablespoons cold-pressed peanut oil
2 tablespoons fresh lime juice
Cayenne pepper to taste
Salt to taste

Combine jícama, peppers, zucchini, and carrot with oil, lime juice, and cayenne pepper. Toss to mix well. (*Note:* May be refrigerated for several hours before serving.) Add salt just before serving.

Makes about 4 cups

THE MANSION
ON TURTLE CREEK
2821 Turtle Creek Boulevard
Dallas, Texas 75219
(214) 559-2100

Lobster-Papaya Quesadillas with Mango Cream

2 ounces fresh goat cheese, crumbled
2 ounces Monterey Jack or Caciotta cheese, grated
1 teaspoon roasted garlic, minced (optional)
4 tablespoons chopped onion
1/2 poblano chili pepper, roasted, peeled, seeded, and diced
1/2 red bell pepper, roasted, peeled, seeded, and diced
1 teaspoon minced cilantro
1/3 teaspoon salt
1 teaspoon fresh lime juice
5 ounces lobster meat, cooked and chopped
1 papaya, peeled, seeded, and chopped
4 (6-inch) flour tortillas, room temperature
2 tablespoons unsalted butter, melted

In a large bowl, combine cheeses and stir in garlic, onion, poblano and bell peppers, cilantro, salt, and lime juice. Next, carefully blend in lobster and papaya. Spread some lobster mixture over half of each tortilla and fold over. Brush each tortilla with melted butter. Heat a large nonstick skillet over medium-high heat and cook quesadillas for about 3 to 4 minutes, until golden brown on both sides. Cut each into 3 triangles and serve with **Mango Cream.**

Serves 4

Mango Cream

2 ripe mangoes, peeled and seeded
1/2 cup sour cream
Juice of 1/2 lemon

Using your hands, squeeze juice from mango pulp into a bowl. Discard juice, transfer pulp to a blender or food processor, and puree until smooth. Add sour cream and lemon juice and blend to incorporate, scraping down sides with a spatula as necessary.

Makes about 1 cup

ROUTH STREET CAFE
formerly at
3005 Routh Street
Dallas, Texas

Salmon Carpaccio

2 pounds fresh salmon fillets
1 (6-ounce) jar capers, drained
2 tablespoons chopped fresh basil
3/4 cup walnut oil
2 tablespoons chopped garlic
1 teaspoon chopped parsley
Salt and pepper to taste
5 lemons

Slice salmon very thin into pieces about the size of your palm. Place slices on a well-chilled plate and keep cold.

In a small bowl, combine capers, basil, oil, garlic, parsley, salt, and pepper. Stir in juice of 1-1/2 lemons. Cut remaining lemons into wedges and reserve.

Coat salmon with oil mixture, using a spoon or pastry brush. Serve within 10 minutes, garnished with lemon wedges.

Serves 10

WATEL'S
1923 McKinney Avenue
Dallas, Texas 75201
(214) 720-0323

Quesadillas with Poblano Peppers and Mushrooms

1 poblano chili pepper, seeded and cut into strips (may substitute a green bell pepper)
5 teaspoons butter, plus additional as needed
Salt and pepper to taste
2 cloves garlic, finely chopped
1 cup mushrooms, sliced
2 cups grated Monterey Jack cheese
6 large flour tortillas

In a small skillet, sauté pepper in 1 teaspoon butter over medium heat until pepper begins to wilt. Lightly season with salt and pepper. Add garlic, 1 teaspoon butter, and mushrooms. Cook until mushrooms begin to release their juices. Remove from heat and set aside.

In a large heavy skillet, melt 1/2 teaspoon butter and swirl in bottom of skillet. Place a flour tortilla in skillet and top with about 1/3 cup grated cheese and 1/4 cup pepper and mushroom mixture. Fold tortilla over and cook on one side until tortilla begins to brown. Turn and cook on the other side until tortilla turns golden and cheese melts. Remove from skillet and keep warm. Repeat with remaining butter, tortillas, cheese, and filling. Cut into wedges to serve.

Serves 6

CHIQUITA MEXICAN CUISINE
4514 Travis Street, Suite 105
Dallas, Texas 75205
(214) 521-0092

Main Courses

Jalapeño Black-Eyed Peas

- 1 pound fresh, frozen, or dried black-eyed peas
- 6 cups water, plus additional as needed
- 2 tablespoons beef base or beef bouillon
- 2 tablespoons Cavender's All-Purpose Seasoning (Greek-style seasoned salt mixture)
- 2 cloves garlic, finely chopped
- 3 fresh jalapeño peppers, seeded and finely chopped
- 1 white onion, finely chopped
- 2 bay leaves
- 1/2 cup chopped red bell pepper
- Cooked rice (8 portions)

Place peas and water in a large saucepan. Stir in beef base, Cavender's seasoning, garlic, jalapeño peppers, onion, and bay leaves. Bring to a boil over high heat, then reduce heat and simmer until peas are tender, about 2-1/2 hours. Add more water during cooking time if needed. Add red bell pepper during the last 20 minutes of cooking time. Serve over rice as a vegetarian main course.

Serves 8

CLARK'S OUTPOST BAR-B-Q RESTAURANT
State Highway 377
Tioga, Texas 76271
(817) 437-2414

Squash and Corn Casserole

3 pounds yellow crookneck squash, cut into 1/2-inch cubes
1 cup whole kernel corn (canned, fresh, or frozen)
1 cup onion, chopped
1 (4-ounce) can chopped green chilies, drained
2 tablespoons butter, melted
1 cup evaporated milk or evaporated skim milk
3 eggs, beaten (may use equivalent amount of egg substitute)
1/2 cup cornbread mix
1/4 teaspoon ground cumin
1 cup grated or cubed American cheese
6–8 dried corn husks (optional; see note)

Combine squash, corn, onion, and chilies and toss well. Beat together butter, eggs, milk, cornbread mix, and cumin. Pour over vegetables and mix gently. Fold in cheese.

Pour mixture into a well-greased 2-quart baking dish and bake at 350 degrees for about 30 minutes, or until hot and bubbly and custard is set.

(*Note:* For a Southwestern presentation, soak 6 to 8 dried corn husks—used to wrap tamales—in warm water overnight. Remove from water, wipe dry, and use to line greased baking dish. Arrange prettiest husks in a sunburst pattern, with ends extending several inches beyond edge of casserole. Pour filling over husks and bake.)

Serves 8

CISCO GRILL
6630 Snider Plaza
Dallas, Texas 75205
(214) 363-9506

▣ Angel Hair Pasta with Goat Cheese Cream Sauce and Sun-Dried Tomatoes

1 cup dry white wine
1/4 cup white wine vinegar
3 shallots, trimmed and minced
2 tablespoons chopped garlic
1/4 teaspoon salt
1/4 teaspoon white pepper
1 bay leaf
3 cups heavy cream
8 ounces goat cheese
1-1/2 pounds angel hair pasta, cooked
4–5 sun-dried tomatoes, softened and sliced thin

In a medium saucepan, combine wine, vinegar, shallots, garlic, salt, pepper, and bay leaf. Bring mixture to a boil, then reduce heat, and simmer for 15 to 20 minutes, or until liquid is reduced by half.

Add cream and bring again to a boil. Reduce heat and simmer for about 4 minutes longer, or until liquid thickens. Remove from heat and strain through a fine sieve.

Transfer sauce to a clean saucepan and warm over low heat. Whisk in goat cheese and simmer for about 10 minutes. (Be careful not to scorch.)

Arrange cooked pasta and sauce on plates and garnish with strips of sun-dried tomatoes.

Serves 4 to 5

BLUE MESA GRILL
5100 Beltline Road, Suite 500
Dallas, Texas 75240
(214) 934-0165

⊠ Angel Hair Pasta with Crabmeat and Roma Tomatoes

1 pound crabmeat, cleaned
4 tablespoons olive oil
2 tablespoons minced garlic
8 Roma tomatoes, diced
1 cup dry white wine
1 pound angel hair pasta, cooked
4 tablespoons butter
2 teaspoons salt
1 teaspoon pepper
1/2 cup Creamy Pesto
Small amount of chicken stock to thin pesto
1/4 cup toasted pine nuts
Whole basil leaves

In a sauté pan, heat oil over medium heat. Add garlic and cook until golden. Remove from heat and immediately stir in tomatoes and crabmeat. Add wine and return pan to heat. Cook until almost all wine has evaporated. Add pasta, butter, salt, and pepper, tossing to coat strands evenly.

Thin **Creamy Pesto** with a small amount of chicken stock, until of a consistency to spoon into streaks or to puddle. Place about 2 tablespoons of pesto on each of 4 plates. Mound pasta over pesto and garnish with toasted pine nuts and basil leaves.

Serves 4

Creamy Pesto

1-1/2 cups fresh basil leaves
2–3 cloves garlic
1/4 cup pine nuts
1/4 cup grated Parmesan cheese
Salt and pepper to taste
1/2 cup chicken stock
2 ounces (4 tablespoons) cream cheese

In a blender or food processor, combine all ingredients except cream cheese. Whirl until smooth, then add cream cheese, 1 tablespoon at a time, until mixture becomes smooth and creamy.

Makes about 1 cup

BEAU NASH
Hotel Crescent Court
400 Crescent Court
Dallas, Texas 75201
(214) 871-3240

Black and White Fettuccine Alfredo

1/2 pound egg fettuccine, cooked al dente
1/2 pound black (squid ink) fettuccine, cooked al dente
1/4 cup olive oil
2 cloves garlic, crushed
3 cups heavy cream
1 cup grated Parmesan cheese
Generous amount of freshly ground pepper
Salt to taste
1/4 cup chopped basil leaves (optional)
1/4 cup chopped parsley (optional)

In a large saucepan, heat olive oil over medium heat. Add garlic and sauté for 10 seconds. Pour in heavy cream and heat until almost boiling, then add Parmesan cheese. Allow liquid to simmer and cook until thickened and reduced by about one-third to one-fourth. Stir in cooked pasta and toss to coat.

Season to taste with pepper and salt, stir in basil and parsley, and serve.

Serves 4

THE FRENCH ROOM
The Adolphus Hotel
1321 Commerce Street
Dallas, Texas 75202
(214) 742-8200

⊠ Springtime Penne with Roasted Garlic, Oven-Dried Cherry Tomatoes, Asparagus, and Goat Cheese

1 cup white wine
2 tablespoons unsalted butter
Salt and pepper to taste
20 thin asparagus spears
20 Oven-Dried Cherry Tomatoes (halves)
1 pound fresh or dried penne pasta, cooked al dente
1/2 cup basil leaves, chopped
1/4 cup extra-virgin olive oil
4 ounces crumbled goat cheese, room temperature

Combine white wine and butter in a large saucepan, and season to taste with salt and pepper. Place pan over high heat and add asparagus. When mixture boils, add **Oven-Dried Cherry Tomatoes** and pulp from head of **Roasted Garlic.** Cook until all but 1/4 cup of liquid has evaporated. Remove from heat. Add cooked pasta to saucepan with tomatoes and garlic, and toss gently. Stir in basil and olive oil. Toss ingredients gently to mix and spoon into 4 bowls. Top each with crumbled goat cheese and serve.

Serves 4

Oven-Dried Cherry Tomatoes

1 pint cherry tomatoes
1/4 cup olive oil

Halve tomatoes horizontally. Arrange on a baking sheet, cut sides up, and drizzle with olive oil. Bake at 350 degrees for about 30 minutes, until tomatoes shrivel and turn light brown around the edges. Remove from oven and reserve. (*Note:* Unused dried tomatoes may be frozen.)

Makes about 30 dried halves

Roasted Garlic

1 head garlic
2 tablespoons olive oil

Slice unpeeled garlic head in half horizontally and place on a sheet of foil, cut sides up. Pour olive oil over halves, then wrap and seal in foil. Poke a few holes in the foil to allow steam to escape. Bake in a 400-degree oven for 45 minutes. When cool enough to handle, squeeze each clove to extract roasted garlic pulp.

PARIGI
3311 Oak Lawn Avenue
Dallas, Texas 75219
(214) 521-0295

Luigi's Seafood Pasta

1 tablespoon olive oil
16 mussels in the shell, scrubbed and debearded
1/2 pound bay scallops, rinsed and dried
1/2 pound baby shrimp, peeled and deveined
4 cloves garlic, finely chopped
1 cup sliced mushrooms
1 cup broccoli florets
3/4 cup dry white wine
1 cup heavy cream
Salt and pepper to taste
1 pound angel hair pasta, cooked

Preheat a large saucepan over medium heat. Add olive oil, mussels, and scallops. When scallops turn white and begin to brown at the edges, add shrimp, garlic, mushrooms, and broccoli. Pour in white wine. When liquid bubbles, cook for about 1 minute more. Gradually add cream, so liquid does not cool much below a simmer. Season to taste with salt and pepper. Discard any mussels that have not opened, add cooked pasta, and toss well to combine and heat through. Adjust seasoning, then serve immediately.

Serves 4

NERO'S ITALIAN
2104 Greenville Avenue
Dallas, Texas 75206
(214) 826-6376

⊠ Cioppino

1/4 cup olive oil
1 cup sliced onions
3/4 cup diced celery
3/4 teaspoon crushed garlic
3/4 pound tomatoes (about 3), peeled, seeded, and chopped
2 teaspoons tomato puree
1 tablespoon chopped parsley
1 tablespoon chopped green onion (white part only)
1 tablespoon chopped green bell pepper
1/4 teaspoon dried oregano
1/8 teaspoon cayenne pepper
1/2 teaspoon salt
1/4 teaspoon pepper
8 hardshell clams, scrubbed well
1/2 pound shrimp, peeled and deveined
3/4 pound boneless cod or sea bass fillet, cut into 2-inch pieces
1-1/4 cups dry white wine
1 cup fish stock or clam juice
1/2 pound crab claws, cooked and shelled
1 steamed lobster tail, cut into 1-inch pieces (optional)

In a large heavy pot, heat olive oil over medium heat. Add onions, celery, and garlic, and sauté just until vegetables begin to wilt. Add tomatoes, tomato puree, parsley, green onion, green pepper, and spices. Cook uncovered over low heat for 30 minutes. Add clams, shrimp, and fish along with white wine and fish stock. Simmer uncovered for 20 minutes. (Do not stir.) Discard any clams that have not opened. Add crab and lobster during last 5 minutes of cooking. Ladle into bowls and serve.

Serves 4

CAFE PACIFIC
24 Highland Park Village
Dallas, Texas 75205
(214) 526-1170

⊠ Fennel-Crusted Tuna with Orange-Ginger Vinaigrette and Crisp Vegetables

8 (7-ounce) tuna steaks
4 tablespoons fennel seeds
3 teaspoons coriander seeds
2 tablespoons white peppercorns
4 egg whites
Salt to taste
1/2 cup olive oil
3 cups shredded green cabbage
1 cup snow peas, sliced on bias
1/2 cup sliced (on bias) green onions (white and green parts)
1/2 cup red bell pepper, cut into thin strips
1/2 cup carrot, sliced
White pepper to taste
2 tablespoons toasted sesame seeds

Rinse tuna steaks and pat dry. Place fennel seeds, coriander seeds, and peppercorns in a clean coffee grinder and process until well blended (or use a mortar and pestle). Transfer to a shallow bowl or small plate.

Whip egg whites until slightly frothy. Season tuna with salt and dip in egg whites. Shake excess egg white from steaks and dip each side in ground spices. Heat 1/4 cup oil in a heavy skillet over medium heat; sear each steak for 2 minutes on each side. Remove from heat and reserve.

Heat remaining 1/4 cup oil in another skillet over medium heat and cook vegetables briefly (2 to 3 minutes), just until well coated with oil and heated through. Season to taste with white pepper and salt. Add sesame seeds and toss to distribute evenly.

Spoon a pool of warm **Orange-Ginger Vinaigrette** in the centers of 8 serving plates and arrange a portion of vegetables on top. Cover with a tuna steak and serve.

Serves 8

Orange-Ginger Vinaigrette

2 cups plus 1 tablespoon olive oil
2 tablespoons peeled and sliced ginger
1/4 cup sliced shallots
4 cloves garlic, sliced
1/2 cup dry sherry
1/2 cup sherry vinegar
2 cups fresh orange juice
1/4 cup Cointreau liqueur
1/2 cup soy sauce
2 sprigs rosemary
2 cups strong chicken stock (regular stock reduced by half)
Salt and pepper to taste

Heat 1 tablespoon olive oil in a skillet or saucepan over medium heat. Add ginger and cook for 1 minute. Add shallots and garlic and cook until softened, about 2 to 3 minutes. Pour in sherry and sherry vinegar and stir to loosen any particles that may be stuck to bottom of pan. Add orange juice, Cointreau, soy sauce, and rosemary. Simmer over low heat until volume is reduced by three-fourths. Add chicken stock and simmer for 3 to 5 minutes more.

Strain vinaigrette through a fine sieve and transfer to a blender. With motor running at low speed, gradually add remaining 2 cups olive oil. Blend until all oil is incorporated. Season with salt and pepper. Serve warm.

Makes about 5 cups

GASPAR'S
150 South Denton Tap Road
Coppell, Texas 75019
(214) 393-5152

Tequila Lime Grilled Shrimp

2 pounds large shrimp, peeled, deveined, and butterflied
2 cups olive oil
1 cup dry white wine
1/2 cup tequila
1/4 cup fresh lime juice
1/4 cup minced garlic
1/4 cup Mexican marigold mint or tarragon, finely chopped
4 teaspoons roasted cumin seeds, ground or crushed fine
2 teaspoons coriander seeds, ground or crushed fine
1/2 teaspoon cayenne pepper
Salt and pepper to taste
6 tablespoons unsalted butter, chilled
Lime slices

Place shrimp in a noncorrosive bowl or resealable plastic bag. In a small bowl or jar with a lid, combine olive oil, wine, tequila, lime juice, garlic, mint, cumin, coriander, cayenne pepper, salt, and pepper. Mix well and pour over shrimp, tossing to coat well. Cover or seal and refrigerate overnight, turning occasionally.

Remove shrimp from marinade, reserving liquid. Transfer reserved marinade to a small saucepan, place over high heat, and simmer until liquid is reduced by half. Remove from heat and whisk in butter, 1 tablespoon at a time, until sauce thickens. Return to heat and keep warm, but do not allow to return to a boil.

Grill shrimp over medium coals for about 5 minutes, turning once. (Do not overcook.) Serve warm with sauce, garnished with lime slices.

Serves 4

BRAZOS
formerly at
2100 Greenville Avenue
Dallas, Texas

Five-Flavor Shrimp

18 medium shrimp, peeled and deveined
1 egg
1/8 teaspoon plus 1/4 teaspoon salt
Dash of white pepper
2 tablespoons cornstarch
2 cups vegetable oil
1/2 green bell pepper, blanched and chopped
8 water chestnuts, chopped
2 green onions, chopped (white and green parts)
3 cloves garlic, finely chopped
2 thin slices of ginger, finely chopped
2 small dried red chili peppers, seeded and chopped
1-1/2 tablespoons ketchup
2 tablespoons sugar
1 tablespoon white vinegar
2 tablespoons chicken broth
1/8 teaspoon Tabasco sauce
Cooked rice (2–4 portions)

Place cleaned shrimp in a medium bowl. Beat together egg, 1/8 teaspoon salt, and white pepper. Pour into bowl with shrimp, tossing to coat evenly. Sprinkle cornstarch over shrimp to coat all sides evenly.

Heat oil in a wok or skillet to 325 degrees. Fry shrimp until golden and crisp, about 2 to 3 minutes. Remove from wok and drain on paper towels. Drop green pepper and water chestnuts in the oil for 10 seconds. Remove, drain, and reserve with shrimp.

Pour off all but 1 tablespoon of oil from wok. Add green onions, garlic, ginger, and dried chili peppers and stir-fry for 15 seconds over medium-high heat. Add ketchup, sugar, 1/4 teaspoon salt, vinegar, chicken broth, and Tabasco sauce. Stir well. When sauce bubbles, return shrimp and vegetables to wok and stir to coat with sauce. Serve warm with rice.

Serves 2 to 4

AUGUST MOON RESTAURANT
15030 Preston Road
Dallas, Texas 75240
(214) 385-7227
2300 North Central Expressway
Plano, Texas 75074
(214) 881-0071

▣ Scampi St. Tropez

16–20 jumbo shrimp, peeled and deveined
Salt and white pepper to taste
Fresh lemon juice to taste
Worcestershire sauce to taste
1 tablespoon butter
2 tablespoons chopped shallots
4 artichoke bottoms, quartered
4 medium mushrooms, quartered
1–2 tablespoons all-purpose flour
3 tablespoons Pernod liqueur
1-1/2 to 2 cups heavy cream
Chopped parsley
Rice pilaf (4 portions)

Season shrimp with salt, white pepper, a drizzle of lemon juice, and several dashes of Worcestershire sauce. Set aside.

Melt butter in a large skillet or sauté pan over medium-high heat. Add shallots and sauté for 2 minutes or until wilted. Add shrimp and cook for 2 to 3 minutes. Add artichokes and mushrooms, then lightly sprinkle with flour.

Next add Pernod. Being very careful (make sure hood fan is off), light liqueur in pan with a match. Allow to burn briefly, then smother flames with a lid, if necessary. Simmer for 3 to 4 minutes. Using a slotted spoon, transfer shrimp, artichokes, and mushrooms to a heated platter and keep warm.

Simmer sauce remaining in pan over medium heat for several minutes longer to thicken. Adjust seasoning to taste. Pour sauce over scampi, sprinkle with chopped parsley, and serve with rice pilaf.

Serves 4

EWALD'S CONTINENTAL RESTAURANT
Stoneleigh Hotel
2927 Maple Avenue
Dallas, Texas 75201
(214) 871-2523

Terlingua Chicken

4 boneless, skinless chicken breasts
8 whole canned jalapeño peppers plus 1/4 cup reserved liquid
2 cups white corn syrup
1/4 teaspoon chili powder
Pinch of ground cumin, or to taste

In a small saucepan, combine jalapeño peppers and reserved liquid, corn syrup, chili powder, and cumin. Bring mixture to a boil, then reduce heat and simmer for 10 minutes.

Remove jalapeños and refrigerate. Cool and refrigerate syrup mixture separately. After cooling, pour 1-1/2 cups syrup mixture over chicken breasts and marinate for 1 hour. Reserve remaining syrup for basting.

Remove chicken from marinade and discard liquid. Over medium coals (preferably mesquite), grill chicken breasts on each side until done, 3 to 5 minutes per side. Baste with reserved syrup mixture during cooking. Transfer to serving plates and garnish with candied jalapeños.

Serves 4

GOOD EATS RESTAURANT
Corporate Offices
3888 Oak Lawn Avenue
Dallas, Texas 75219
(214) 522-0570
Several locations

Pollo Pizziolla

- 8 boneless, skinless chicken breasts
- 1 cup all-purpose flour
- Salt and pepper to taste
- 1/2 cup olive oil
- 3 tablespoons chopped garlic
- 2 (24-ounce) cans plum tomatoes, drained and cut into 1/2-inch pieces
- 1-1/2 teaspoons dried oregano
- 3 tablespoons finely chopped parsley

Trim fat from chicken breasts, rinse in cold water, and pat dry with paper towels. Season flour generously with salt and pepper, mixing well, and spread onto a plate or piece of waxed paper. Dip chicken breasts in flour to lightly coat all sides.

Heat olive oil in a large skillet over medium-high heat. Place chicken breasts in a single layer in skillet along with garlic. Fry until chicken becomes golden around the edges, then turn and cook the other side. Stir in tomatoes and oregano, and cook uncovered for 10 minutes. Sprinkle with fresh parsley and serve immediately.

Serves 8

MASSIMO DA MILANO
5519 West Lovers Lane
Dallas, Texas 75209
(214) 351-1426
Several locations

Chicken Mango Curry

2 pounds boneless, skinless chicken breasts, cut into bite-sized pieces
1 cup all-purpose flour
2 tablespoons vegetable oil
1 large red onion, chopped
1 red bell pepper, diced
1 green bell pepper, diced
2 jalapeño peppers, seeded and diced
1 tablespoon chopped garlic
1 tablespoon curry powder
3 cups chicken stock
1 mango, peeled, seeded, and diced
1/2 cup canned coconut milk
3 cups cooked rice or couscous
Condiments: chutney, sliced green onions, crisply cooked crumbled bacon, chopped jalapeño peppers

Combine chicken and 1/2 cup flour in a plastic bag. Shake to coat all pieces evenly, then remove chicken and shake off excess flour.

Heat oil over medium heat in a large, deep, ovenproof skillet with a tight-fitting lid. Fry chicken pieces until lightly browned, about 10 minutes. Cook in two batches, if needed, so pieces are not too crowded and brown nicely. Add onion, bell peppers, and jalapeño peppers to skillet and sauté for about 5 minutes, stirring frequently. Add garlic and curry powder, and cook for 5 minutes more.

In a small bowl, whisk together 1/2 cup flour and chicken stock, stirring to eliminate all lumps. Add to skillet along with mango and coconut milk. Bring liquid to a simmer, cover skillet with lid, and place in a 350-degree oven for 1 hour. Serve over rice or couscous and offer a variety of condiments.

Serves 4 to 6

very good!

CITY CAFE
5757 West Lovers Lane
Dallas, Texas 75209
(214) 351-2233

Braised Leg of Lamb Abruzzi

1 (2-pound) leg of lamb, boned and tied
1/4 pound lean salt pork, rind removed
3 cloves garlic, cut into slivers
6 sprigs rosemary
Salt to taste
6 tablespoons oil
1 cup dry white wine
1-1/2 pounds tomatoes, peeled, seeded, chopped, and drained
2 tablespoons chopped parsley
1 tablespoon chopped oregano
Pepper to taste

Rinse and dry leg of lamb; set aside.

Chop salt pork and boil for 10 minutes. Transfer to a skillet and sauté over medium heat, stirring occasionally, until pieces are golden. Remove pork with a slotted spoon, drain on paper towels, and reserve.

Make small slits in lamb and insert slivers of garlic and pieces of rosemary. Rub lamb with salt. Heat oil in a Dutch oven over medium heat. Add lamb and brown on all sides. Pour wine over lamb and simmer until almost all liquid has evaporated. Add tomatoes, reserved salt pork, parsley, oregano, and enough water to come about one-third up the sides of the lamb. Season with salt and pepper. Bring to a boil, then cover, reduce heat, and simmer for about 2 hours, or until lamb is fork tender. Transfer lamb to a hot serving platter and keep warm.

Return pot to heat and simmer for about 5 minutes to reduce sauce. Adjust seasoning, pour over lamb, and serve.

Serves 6

CAPRICCIO
2515 McKinney Avenue, Suite 125
Dallas, Texas 75201
(214) 871-2004

⊠ Lamb Shanks Provençale

4 lamb shanks
1 carrot, peeled and chopped
2 stalks celery, chopped
1 onion, chopped, plus 1/2 cup additional
2 tablespoons olive oil
About 2 cups chicken broth
Salt to taste
4 large tomatoes, peeled and chopped
4 cloves garlic, chopped
2 tablespoons chopped fresh basil or 1 teaspoon dried
3 tablespoons butter
1 tablespoon chopped parsley

Place lamb shanks in a roasting pan with carrot, celery, and 1 chopped onion. Sprinkle with 1 tablespoon olive oil and roast in a 350-degree oven for 30 minutes. Remove from oven and add enough chicken broth to fill half the pan. Cover and roast lamb shanks for 1 hour longer, basting or turning occasionally. Season with salt and keep warm.

In a saucepan, sauté 1/2 cup chopped onion in 1 tablespoon olive oil until wilted, about 3 minutes. Add 2 cloves chopped garlic and stir. (Be careful not to burn.) Add tomatoes, basil, and salt to taste. Bring to a boil, then remove from heat and keep warm.

In another small saucepan, melt butter and add remaining 2 cloves chopped garlic and parsley. Remove from heat when butter starts to foam. Serve shanks on bed of sauce, drizzled with garlic-parsley butter.

Serves 4

LE CAVISTE
formerly at
5405 West Lovers Lane
Dallas, Texas

Sautéed Calf's Liver with Bacon, Onions, and Roasted Garlic Mashed Potatoes

1-1/2 pounds calf's liver, thinly sliced
12 slices thick slab bacon, coarsely chopped
1 cup all-purpose flour, seasoned to taste with salt and pepper
2 cups sliced yellow onion

In a large heavy skillet over high heat, fry bacon until crisp. Remove from skillet and drain on paper towels; keep warm. Pour off all but a thin coating of fat from pan, about 3 tablespoons.

Dip liver slices in seasoned flour to coat. Over medium heat, cook liver briefly on both sides, about 30 to 60 seconds or until just slightly pink inside. Remove from pan and keep warm. Add onion to pan and sauté until soft and brown, about 7 to 10 minutes. Add bacon and stir to coat. Top liver slices generously with onion and bacon mixture, and serve with **Roasted Garlic Mashed Potatoes.**

Serves 6

Roasted Garlic Mashed Potatoes

1 head garlic, broken into individual cloves and peeled
2 tablespoons olive oil
1/2 cup chicken stock
2 pounds (about 6 medium) russet potatoes, peeled and cut into 1-inch cubes
1 cup heavy cream
1/2 cup (1 stick) butter
Salt and white pepper to taste

Place garlic and olive oil in a small sauté pan over medium heat. Sauté, stirring frequently, until garlic cloves turn golden brown. Remove from heat and allow to cool. Transfer cooled garlic cloves along with chicken stock to a blender or food processor and whirl until smooth and creamy, similar to the consistency of mayonnaise. (*Note:* May be made ahead and refrigerated for 1 week, or frozen for longer storage.)

Place potatoes in a heavy saucepan with enough water to cover. Bring to a boil and simmer until potatoes are tender, about 15 to 20 minutes.

Combine cream and butter in a small saucepan. Heat to melt butter, then keep warm.

When potatoes are easily pierced with a fork, drain and return to pan. Place over low heat for several minutes to dry potatoes, occasionally shaking pan vigorously. Run potatoes through a food mill and combine with cream and butter mixture to achieve desired consistency. Potatoes may be mashed with a masher or whipped with an electric mixer, although texture will not be as smooth. Season to taste with roasted garlic puree, salt, and pepper.

Serves 6

NANA GRILL
Loews Anatole Hotel
2201 Stemmons Freeway
Dallas, Texas 75207
(214) 748-1200

⊠ Veal Nero's

2 pounds veal scallops
1/4 cup olive oil
1/2 pound peeled crawfish tail meat
Salt to taste
1/2 teaspoon white pepper
1/2 teaspoon cayenne pepper
1 tablespoon chopped shallots
1/4 cup dry sherry
3/4 cup heavy cream
Steamed vegetables or pasta

Rinse veal pieces and pat dry. Heat olive oil in a heavy skillet or sauté pan over medium heat. Add veal and sauté for 2 to 3 minutes on each side. Remove from skillet and keep warm. Add crawfish tails to pan and sauté for 1 to 2 minutes, then remove from skillet and keep warm. Season veal and crawfish with salt and peppers.

Place shallots in pan and cook briefly, about 1 minute. Add sherry and simmer for 1 minute. Stir to loosen any particles from bottom of pan. Add heavy cream and simmer for 1 minute. Return veal and crawfish to pan and adjust seasonings to taste.

Arrange veal slices on serving plates and garnish with a crawfish tail and sauce. Serve with steamed vegetables or pasta on the side.

Serves 4

NERO'S ITALIAN
2104 Greenville Avenue
Dallas, Texas 75206
(214) 826-6376

⊠ Rahmschnitzel

8 (1-1/2 to 2-ounce) veal cutlet pieces, pounded thin
2-1/2 teaspoons Dijon mustard
1 cup all-purpose flour
4 tablespoons butter
1/2 teaspoon finely chopped shallots
1/2 cup dry white wine
2 cups heavy cream
1 tablespoon drained capers
Salt and pepper to taste
Minced parsley
Spaetzle or cooked noodles (optional)

Brush veal on both sides with 2 teaspoons mustard and lightly sprinkle with flour. Set aside on waxed paper.

Melt butter in a skillet over medium-high heat. When bubbly, add veal and sauté on both sides until golden, about 1 minute per side. Remove from skillet and keep warm.

Add shallots to skillet and stir briefly. Add wine, stirring to scrape up any pieces of meat or flour stuck to pan. Cook until wine is reduced to about 2 tablespoons. Add cream and capers. Bring mixture to a boil and reduce heat to simmer. Season with salt and pepper, then add remaining 1/2 teaspoon mustard. Return veal with any accumulated juices to skillet and simmer for 3 to 4 minutes. Garnish with fresh minced parsley and serve with spaetzle or noodles, if desired.

Serves 4

BELVEDERE
Crest Park Hotel
4242 Lomo Alto
Dallas, Texas 75219
(214) 528-6510

Ewald's Veal Steak "Au Moulin"

8 (2-1/2-ounce) veal medallions
Salt and white pepper to taste
2 eggs, beaten
1 cup all-purpose flour
1 tablespoon plus 1-1/2 teaspoons clarified butter (see instructions on p. 28)
1/2 pound mushrooms, sliced
1 tablespoon chopped onion
1 tablespoon chopped parsley
Juice of 1/2 lemon
1/4 cup cognac
1/3 cup dry white wine
1 cup heavy cream

Gently pound veal medallions to flatten slightly. Season with salt and white pepper. Dip veal in egg, then flour, shaking off excess. Heat clarified butter in large sauté pan or skillet and sauté veal over medium heat for about 3 minutes on each side.

Add mushrooms, onion, and parsley. Sauté for a few minutes, then add lemon juice and cognac to pan. Being very careful (make sure hood fan is off), flame cognac by lighting pan juices with a match. Allow to burn briefly, smothering flames with a lid, if necessary.

Add wine and cream, and simmer for about 2 minutes. Remove veal and arrange on a serving platter; keep warm. Continue to simmer sauce until it thickens slightly. Adjust seasoning to taste, pour sauce over veal, and serve.

Serves 4

EWALD'S CONTINENTAL RESTAURANT
Stoneleigh Hotel
2927 Maple Avenue
Dallas, Texas 75201
(214) 871-2523

Osso Buco Milanese

8 pounds veal shanks, cut into 3-inch pieces
2 cups all-purpose flour
3/4 cup vegetable oil
3/4 cup (1-1/2 sticks) butter
1 cup finely chopped yellow onion
2/3 cup finely chopped carrots
2/3 cup finely chopped celery
1 large clove garlic, chopped
Grated zest of 1 lemon
1-1/2 cups dry white wine
2 to 2-1/2 cups veal or chicken broth, or as needed
2 cups canned, drained plum tomatoes
1 teaspoon chopped thyme
2 teaspoons Italian parsley
1/4 cup basil leaves, torn into pieces
1 tablespoon salt, or to taste
1 teaspoon crushed red pepper

Preheat oven to 350 degrees. Coat veal shanks in flour, shaking to remove excess. Heat vegetable oil over medium-high heat in a large, heavy, ovenproof Dutch oven with a tight-fitting lid. Cook shanks, turning frequently, to brown all sides. Remove from pot and set aside.

Add butter to pot, then onion, carrots, and celery. Reduce heat to medium and simmer vegetables until very soft, about 10 minutes. Stir in garlic and lemon zest, and simmer for 2 to 3 minutes more. Add white wine, stirring to loosen any bits stuck to the bottom. When liquid begins to bubble, simmer for 3 to 5 minutes until liquid is reduced slightly and the alcohol burns off the wine. Return shanks to pot and pour in just enough broth to cover. Add tomatoes, thyme, parsley, basil, salt, and crushed red pepper. Bring liquid to a boil, then remove from heat, cover, and bake for 1-1/2 to 2 hours, turning shanks and basting with pan liquid every 30 minutes.

Shanks are done when meat is fork tender and almost falls off the bone. Sauce should be thickened and creamy.

Serves 4 to 6

MI PIACI
14854 Montfort
Dallas, Texas 75240
(214) 934-8424

Hard Rock Chili

5 pounds coarsely ground beef
3 cups coarsely chopped yellow onion
2 cups coarsely chopped green bell pepper
3 cloves garlic, finely chopped
6 cups water
2 cups tomato paste
4-1/2 tablespoons chili powder
2-1/4 tablespoons ground cumin
2-1/4 tablespoons salt
3/4 tablespoon white pepper
2-1/2 tablespoons ground oregano
3/4 tablespoon cayenne pepper
2 (15-ounce) cans diced tomatoes, undrained
2 (15-ounce) cans kidney beans, undrained

In a large pot, brown meat in batches over medium-high heat. Drain fat, add onions, green pepper, and garlic, and cook for 5 minutes.

In a separate bowl, combine water, tomato paste, chili powder, cumin, salt, white pepper, oregano, and cayenne pepper, then add to meat mixture. Bring chili to a boil, then lower heat and simmer for 30 minutes. Stir in tomatoes and kidney beans, and simmer for 15 to 30 minutes more, until meat is tender.

Serves 10

HARD ROCK CAFE
2601 McKinney Avenue
Dallas, Texas 75204
(214) 855-0007

Grilled Beef Chop with Roquefort Apple-Bacon Butter

4 (10- to 12-ounce) bone-in beef loin chops, room temperature
Kosher salt and cracked pepper to taste

Season chops with salt and pepper, then grill over hot coals until medium-rare, about 10 to 15 minutes, turning once. Serve each chop topped with 1 to 2 tablespoons **Roquefort Apple-Bacon Butter.**

Serves 4

Roquefort Apple-Bacon Butter

10 to 12 shallots, peeled
1 pound (4 sticks) plus 1–2 tablespoons butter, softened
1 cup cooked and crumbled apple-smoked bacon (or other top quality bacon)
1 cup crumbled Roquefort cheese
2 tablespoons chopped chives
2 tablespoons Worcestershire sauce
Salt and cracked pepper to taste

Melt 1 to 2 tablespoons butter in a small skillet. Add shallots and cook over medium heat until shallots begin to brown or caramelize. Transfer shallots and butter to a large sheet of aluminum foil. Wrap tightly so butter cannot leak and place packet in a 350-degree oven for 15 minutes. Remove from oven, but do not open foil; allow to cool. Mash cooled shallots to a smooth consistency and combine with 1 pound butter, bacon, Roquefort cheese, chives, Worcestershire sauce, salt, and pepper. Chill to set before serving, and refrigerate unused portions.

Makes about 4 cups

CHAPLIN'S
1928 Greenville Avenue
Dallas, Texas 75206
(214) 823-3300

Roasted Beef Tenderloin with Rutabaga-Potato Gratin

3 pounds center-cut beef tenderloin, trimmed
1 teaspoon dried basil
1 teaspoon dried oregano
1/2 teaspoon dried rosemary
1 teaspoon minced garlic
1 teaspoon cracked pepper
4 teaspoons olive oil
1-1/2 teaspoons salt

Rinse tenderloin and pat dry. In a small bowl, combine basil, oregano, rosemary, garlic, pepper, and 2 teaspoons olive oil. Rub tenderloin with mixture and let sit at room temperature for 30 minutes (or refrigerate for 2 to 3 hours). Season with salt and set aside.

Preheat oven to 350 degrees. In an oven-proof skillet, heat remaining 2 teaspoons olive oil and sear tenderloin on all sides to a deep brown color. Transfer skillet with tenderloin to oven and roast for approximately 18 to 20 minutes for medium-rare. Remove from oven and let tenderloin sit for 5 to 10 minutes, allowing juices to settle. Reheat just before serving, then slice. Serve with **Rutabaga-Potato Gratin.**

Serves 6 to 8

Rutabaga-Potato Gratin

- 1 pound rutabagas, peeled and sliced 1/4-inch thick
- 1 pound potatoes, peeled and sliced 1/4-inch thick
- 1 teaspoon olive oil
- 1/2 cup chopped onion
- 2 teaspoons minced garlic
- 3 cups heavy cream
- 1 teaspoon salt, or to taste
- 1 teaspoon pepper
- 1 teaspoon minced rosemary
- 1/2 cup shredded Parmesan cheese

Grease a 10-by-12-by-2-inch pan with olive oil or nonstick spray. Layer half the rutabagas, then half the potatoes, in pan. (Slices should be dry.) Add a layer of remaining rutabaga slices and top with remaining potatoes.

Preheat oven to 350 degrees. Heat olive oil in a saucepan over medium heat and add onion and garlic. Sauté just until soft. Add cream, salt, pepper, and rosemary. Bring to a boil, reduce heat, then simmer for 4 to 5 minutes or until reduced by one-third. Pour sauce over layered vegetables, then sprinkle with Parmesan cheese. Cover and bake for 45 minutes, then uncover and bake for 20 minutes more. Cool to room temperature and cut into squares. Reheat to serve.

Serves 8

DAKOTA'S
600 North Akard Street
Dallas, Texas 75201
(214) 740-4001

⊠ Uncle Tai's Beef

- 1-1/2 pounds flank steak
- 2/3 cup plus 3 tablespoons water
- 1/2 teaspoon baking soda
- 1/4 teaspoon salt
- 3 tablespoons dry sherry or shao hsing wine
- 1 egg white
- 3-1/2 tablespoons cornstarch
- 4 cups plus 2 tablespoons peanut, vegetable, or corn oil
- 2 green onions, cut into 1/2-inch pieces (about 1/3 cup)
- 3 tablespoons dried orange peel (available at Asian groceries and spice stores, or see note)
- 3 thin slices ginger, cut into 1/2-inch pieces
- 1 hot red chili pepper, chopped (optional)
- 3 tablespoons soy sauce
- 2 tablespoons sugar
- 1 teaspoon sesame oil
- 1/4 cup chicken broth
- 10 dried red chili peppers

Chill flank steak in the freezer for about 30 minutes for easier handling. Place icy, but not frozen, steak on a flat surface and, holding a sharp knife parallel to the beef, slice it in half widthwise. Cut each half into very thin strips, about 1/4 inch each. (There should be about 4 cups loosely packed beef strips.) Place beef in a large bowl and add 2/3 cup water blended with baking soda. Refrigerate overnight or for at least 1 hour.

Just before cooking, rinse the beef thoroughly under cold running water. Drain, pat dry, and return to a bowl. Add salt, 1 tablespoon sherry, and egg white to meat strips. Stir in a circular motion until egg white becomes bubbly. Add 1-1/2 tablespoons cornstarch and 2 tablespoons oil; stir to blend. Set aside.

Combine green onions, orange peel, ginger, and fresh red chili pepper. Set aside.

Combine remaining 2 tablespoons sherry, soy sauce, sugar, remaining 2 tablespoons cornstarch blended with remaining 3 tablespoons water, sesame oil, and chicken broth. Stir to blend.

Heat 4 cups of oil in a wok or skillet, and when it is almost smoking, add beef. Fry for about 45 seconds, stirring constantly, and remove with slotted spoon or wire scoop. Drain meat well and set aside briefly.

Return meat to wok and fry again in same hot oil over high heat for about 15 seconds, stirring. Drain once more. Return meat to hot oil a third time and fry for about 15 seconds, stirring. Drain meat again.

Drain oil from wok, reserving about 2 tablespoons. Add dried chili peppers, stirring over high heat until brown and almost blackened, about 30 seconds. Remove peppers and discard. Add green onion mixture and stir. Add beef and cook, stirring constantly, for about 10 seconds. Add wine mixture, stirring, and cook for about 15 seconds until hot and meat is well coated. Serve warm.

(*Note:* To make dried orange peel, remove peel from an orange and eliminate as much white pith as possible. Cut peel into strips, arrange on a baking sheet, and dry in a 200-degree oven for about 1 hour. Store in an airtight container.)

Serves 4

UNCLE TAI'S HUNAN YUAN
13350 Dallas Parkway, Suite 3370
Dallas, Texas 75240
(214) 934-9998

Japanese Eggplants and Pork in Garlic Sauce

- 2 whole Japanese eggplants, unpeeled
- 2 cups corn oil
- 2 ounces (1/4 cup) ground pork
- 2 cloves garlic, finely chopped
- 2 green onions, chopped (white and green parts)
- 1 tablespoon dry sherry
- 1-1/2 tablespoons soy sauce
- 2-1/2 tablespoons sugar
- 1 tablespoon white vinegar
- 1/3 teaspoon Tabasco sauce
- 1/3 cup chicken broth
- 1 tablespoon cornstarch dissolved in 1 tablespoon water
- 1/3 teaspoon sesame oil
- 1 tablespoon chopped cilantro leaves

Remove stem ends from eggplants. Halve each eggplant lengthwise, then cut into 1-1/2-inch pieces. Heat corn oil in a wok or large skillet to 325 degrees. Place eggplant in hot oil and fry until soft, about 3 to 4 minutes.

Have a pot of boiling water ready. When eggplant is soft, transfer from wok to hot water and immerse. Quickly remove pieces with a slotted spoon and put into a colander to drain.

Pour off all but 2 tablespoons oil from wok. Over medium-high heat, fry ground pork in oil until it begins to lose its pink color. Add garlic and green onions, and stir-fry for 15 seconds. Add dry sherry. Stir in soy sauce, sugar, vinegar, Tabasco sauce, and chicken broth. When sauce boils, drizzle in some dissolved cornstarch, stirring constantly until sauce begins to thicken and desired consistency is achieved. (Not all cornstarch may be needed.)

Return eggplants to wok, stirring well to coat evenly with sauce. Just before serving, sprinkle sesame oil over mixture and garnish with cilantro.

Serves 4

AUGUST MOON RESTAURANT
15030 Preston Road
Dallas, Texas 75240
(214) 385-7227
2300 North Central Expressway
Plano, Texas 75074
(214) 881-0071

Roast Pork Loin with Pecan-Sage Sauce

1 (1-1/2-pound) boneless pork loin, with fat
1–2 tablespoons chopped sage, or to taste
1 tablespoon minced garlic, or to taste
1–2 teaspoons dried thyme, or to taste
Salt and cracked pepper to taste
Polenta (4 portions)

Preheat oven to 350 degrees. Rub pork with sage, garlic, thyme, salt, and pepper. Place in a shallow pan and roast for about 25 minutes per pound, or until meat registers 160 degrees on a meat thermometer. Slice thin and serve with **Pecan-Sage Sauce**, alongside squares of polenta.

Serves 4

Pecan-Sage Sauce

1 tablespoon butter
1/2 cup pecan halves
1 teaspoon chopped garlic
1 teaspoon chopped shallot
1/4 cup Madeira wine
2-1/2 cups veal demi-glace or canned beef gravy
1 tablespoon chopped sage
Salt and pepper to taste

Melt butter in a skillet and add pecans, garlic, and shallot. Cook briefly, then add wine. Stir in demi-glace and simmer over medium heat until liquid is thickened and reduced by about one-third. Add sage and adjust seasoning to taste.

Makes about 2 cups

BLUE MESA GRILL
5100 Beltline Road, Suite 500
Dallas, Texas 75240
(214) 934-0165

Slovenian Cabbage Rolls with Paprika Sauce

1 large head green cabbage
1 teaspoon vegetable oil
1/2 onion, finely chopped
2 cloves garlic, finely chopped
1/2 pound lean ground chuck
1/2 pound lean ground pork
1-1/2 cups cooked white rice
1 egg, lightly beaten
Salt and pepper to taste
1/2 teaspoon dried marjoram
1/2 teaspoon dried thyme
1 cup sour cream, or to taste

Remove core of cabbage with a boning knife. Insert prongs of a large meat fork into cabbage and place head into a large pot of boiling, salted water. Simmer for about 5 to 7 minutes to blanch, occasionally twirling cabbage with fork. Cabbage is properly blanched when leaves begin to separate when twirled.

When leaves are slightly softened, remove cabbage from water and drain. Cool slightly, then select 8 to 10 large, pretty leaves. Remove any remaining core by cutting a small "V" out of core end. Reserve remaining cabbage.

In a small sauté pan, heat oil and add onion and garlic. Sauté over medium-high heat until onion becomes soft and translucent. Remove from heat and reserve.

In a large bowl, combine beef, pork, rice, egg, salt, pepper, marjoram, thyme, cooked onions, and garlic. Using hands, mix well. Place approximately 1/3 cup of mixture into the center of each selected cabbage leaf. Arrange meat horizontally and fold sides of leaves over meat. Roll from core end toward the top, so that outer rim of leaf is on outer part of the roll. Rolls should be 3 to 4 inches long.

Place cabbage rolls in a 9-by-13-inch roasting pan. Chop remaining cabbage leaves and sprinkle over rolls. Stir **Paprika Sauce** well and pour over rolls, making sure sauce spreads to bottom of pan. Cover pan with foil and bake in a 350-degree oven for 30 to 45 minutes, or until cabbage is tender and meat is cooked through.

Remove baking pan from oven and add sour cream by teaspoonfuls, blending gently to soften flavor and color, as desired.

Serves 4

Paprika Sauce

5 strips bacon, chopped
1/2 onion, finely chopped
2 cloves garlic, finely chopped
1 bay leaf
Pinch of dried thyme
2 tablespoons tomato paste
2 tablespoons paprika
2–3 cups water
1 tablespoon cornstarch dissolved in 1 tablespoon cold water
Salt and pepper to taste

In a medium saucepan, sauté bacon over medium heat until it begins to brown. Add onion and garlic, sautéing until vegetables become soft and bacon is brown. Add bay leaf, thyme, tomato paste, and paprika. Add 2 cups water, stirring to eliminate any lumps of tomato paste and paprika. Simmer for about 10 minutes, then stir in cornstarch and simmer for several minutes more over low heat to thicken. Adjust consistency with additional water as desired. Season with salt and pepper. Simmer for several minutes more, until desired flavor and consistency are achieved.

Makes 2 to 3 cups

FRANKI'S LI'L EUROPE
362 Casa Linda Plaza
Dallas, Texas 75218
(214) 320-0426

⊠ Venison Medallions with Sweet Potato Puree and Brown Butter Spinach

8 (3-ounce) venison loin medallions
2 tablespoons olive oil, plus additional as needed
Salt to taste
2 teaspoons cayenne pepper
2 teaspoons white pepper
2 teaspoons black pepper

Rub medallions with olive oil and sprinkle both sides of meat with salt. Combine cayenne, white, and black peppers in a small bowl and use to sprinkle over both sides of medallions.

Grill venison over hot coals or sauté in a small amount of oil over high heat for about 2 to 3 minutes per side, or to desired doneness. (Venison is best cooked no more than medium rare.) Set aside and keep warm until ready to serve.

Place 2 venison medallions on each of 4 serving plates, over a bed of **Brown Butter Spinach.** Garnish with dollops of **Sweet Potato Puree** or pipe puree onto each plate.

Serves 4

Brown Butter Spinach

1 (10-ounce) bag fresh spinach
4 tablespoons salted butter
4 cloves garlic, finely chopped
Salt and pepper to taste

Soak spinach in salted water to remove any sand particles. Rinse and drain. Tear off tough stems, shake off excess water, and dry with paper towels.

Melt butter in a large skillet over medium-high heat. Cook until butter foams and turns amber. Add spinach and stir for 30 to 45 seconds, or just until leaves begin to wilt. Add garlic and season to taste with salt and pepper. Remove from heat and serve.

Serves 4

Sweet Potato Puree

2 large sweet potatoes, peeled and quartered
Salt to taste
2 tablespoons salted butter
Pepper to taste

Place potatoes in a small saucepan with enough water to cover. Season with salt to taste. Bring to a boil over high heat and cook until potatoes are tender, about 15 minutes. Drain potatoes and place in a blender or food processor. Whirl with butter, salt, and pepper until smooth. (*Note:* May be made ahead and reheated just before serving.)

Makes about 2 cups

LAUREL'S
Sheraton Park Central Hotel
12720 Merit Drive
Dallas, Texas 75251
(214) 852-2021

Rabbit Fricassee

3 rabbits, skinned and cut into serving pieces
6 slices bacon, chopped
1 large onion, chopped
20 mushrooms, sliced
1-1/4 cups white wine
2-1/2 cups beef bouillon
Salt and pepper to taste
1 teaspoon Dijon mustard
1/4 cup heavy cream

Rinse rabbit pieces and pat dry. Place bacon in a large skillet or Dutch oven. Cook over high heat for 3 minutes, until bacon begins to release fat. Add rabbit pieces and sauté (in batches if necessary) until meat begins to brown. Turn to brown both sides. When all pieces have been browned, return to skillet along with any accumulated juices.

Add onions and mushrooms and sauté for 2 minutes. Add wine and bouillon, then season to taste with salt and pepper. Reduce heat, cover, and simmer for 20 minutes or until rabbit is tender. Stir in mustard and cream, simmer for 2 minutes longer, and serve.

Serves 8

WATEL'S
1923 McKinney Avenue
Dallas, Texas 75201
(214) 720-0323

Sweet Endings

Eggnog Crème Brûlée

2-1/2 cups heavy cream
3/4 cup sugar
1/4 cup firmly packed brown sugar
1-1/2 teaspoons nutmeg
5 egg yolks
3 tablespoons brandy
1 tablespoon vanilla extract

Preheat oven to 300 degrees. Butter a 1-1/2-quart baking dish and set aside.

Place cream in a medium saucepan and bring to a boil over medium-high heat. Remove from heat. In a small bowl, combine 1/4 cup sugar, brown sugar, and 1 teaspoon nutmeg. Set aside

In another small bowl, combine 1/2 cup sugar, egg yolks, brandy, vanilla, and remaining 1/2 teaspoon nutmeg. Using an electric mixer, beat until fluffy, scraping sides of bowl once. Slowly add 1 cup hot cream, stirring constantly. When well blended, add remaining cream and mix thoroughly. Pour mixture into prepared baking dish.

Sit baking dish in a larger pan and pour in enough hot water to come up 1 inch around the outside of the baking dish. Place in oven and bake until custard is just set around the edge, about 1 hour. Cool and refrigerate 6 hours.

Sprinkle reserved sugar mixture over custard and place 6 to 8 inches under a hot broiler until the sugar melts and caramelizes. Serve.

Serves 8

LAUREL'S
Sheraton Park Central Hotel
12720 Merit Drive
Dallas, Texas 75251
(214) 851-2021

Bailey's Pecan Crème Brûlée in Pecan Tart Shells

2 cups heavy cream
1/2 vanilla bean
1/4 cup coarsely chopped pecans
6 egg yolks
1/3 cup sugar
2 tablespoons Bailey's Irish Cream liqueur
4–6 tablespoons firmly packed brown sugar

Place cream in a heavy saucepan along with vanilla bean and chopped pecans. Bring to a boil, then remove from heat and allow to cool slightly.

In a bowl, beat egg yolks and sugar until smooth and light yellow. Add a small amount of cream to yolks and stir. Gradually stir yolks into slightly cooled cream. Return saucepan to low heat and cook until custard thickens enough to coat the back of a spoon. Stir in Bailey's Irish Cream.

Strain custard through a sieve and cool in a shallow bowl. Fill **Pecan Tart Shells** with cooled custard. Sprinkle each with 1 tablespoon brown sugar and place under preheated broiler just until brown sugar melts. (Be careful to avoid burning.)

Serves 4 to 6

Pecan Tart Shells

2 cups all-purpose flour
3/4 cup (1-1/2 sticks) butter
1/2 cup finely ground pecans
Pinch of salt
2 tablespoons cold water, or enough to moisten dough

Place flour, butter, ground pecans, and salt in a food processor. Pulse briefly until mixture becomes the consistency of cornmeal. Add water and process just enough so that dough holds together. Form dough into a ball, cover, and refrigerate for 30 minutes.

Roll dough into 6-inch rounds and use to line 4 to 6 (4-inch) molds or tart pans. Trim edges and chill in refrigerator for 30 minutes. Preheat oven to 450 degrees. Prick bottom of shells and bake for 8 to 10 minutes or until lightly browned. Cool before filling.

Makes 4 to 6 shells

LAUREL'S
Sheraton Park Central Hotel
12720 Merit Drive
Dallas, Texas 75251
(214) 851-2021

Zuppa di Mascarpone

1 pint strawberries
1 pint raspberries
1 pint blueberries
1/4 cup fresh lemon juice
1/2 cup plus 6 heaping tablespoons sugar
1/2 cup Grand Marnier liqueur
6 eggs yolks (or equivalent egg substitute)
1 pound mascarpone (Italian cream cheese), softened
6 egg whites
24 ladyfingers

Rinse berries. Remove stems from strawberries. Combine berries with lemon juice, 1/2 cup sugar, and Grand Marnier. Gently toss to mix ingredients and allow to sit at room temperature for 1 to 2 hours.

Beat egg yolks and 6 tablespoons sugar well, until mixture turns light yellow. Add mascarpone and stir lightly. Beat egg whites until stiff and gently fold into mascarpone mixture. Drain berry juices and reserve in separate bowl. Dip ladyfingers into berry juices briefly just to moisten. Arrange ladyfingers in one layer on the bottom and up the sides of a serving bowl.

Spoon about one-third of the mascarpone mixture on top of the ladyfingers. Spoon one-third of the berries onto the mascarpone and repeat, layering with moistened ladyfingers, mascarpone, and berries until all are used. Cover with plastic wrap and refrigerate for at least 1 hour before serving.

Serves 12

THE MOZZARELLA COMPANY
2944 Elm Street
Dallas, Texas 75226
(214) 741-4072

Apple, Prune, and Walnut Custard Soufflé with Caramel Sauce

6 tablespoons unsalted butter, melted
6 (1-inch) slices egg bread, such as challah (about 6 ounces)
2 cups cored, peeled, and sliced tart green apples
6 large eggs
2/3 cup sugar
1/2 teaspoon salt
2-1/2 cups half-and-half
2 teaspoons vanilla extract
1 teaspoon ginger
1/2 cup chopped walnuts, lightly toasted
1 cup chopped pitted prunes

Preheat oven to 350 degrees. Brush one side of bread slices with 4 tablespoons butter and set aside. Place remaining 2 tablespoons in a small sauté pan, and cook apple slices over medium-high heat until light brown. Set aside and cool.

In a large bowl, beat together eggs, sugar, and salt. Heat half-and-half in a saucepan over medium heat until scalded or a film forms around the edge. Remove from heat, cool slightly, and stir about 1/4 cup scalded half-and-half into egg mixture. Slowly stir egg mixture into half-and-half; add vanilla and ginger. Allow to cool slightly.

Lightly grease an 8-cup soufflé dish. Create layers of bread, walnuts, prunes, and sautéed apples in the dish, ending with apples. Pour egg mixture over layered ingredients and allow to sit for 30 minutes.

Set soufflé dish in a larger baking pan. Pour in enough hot water to come halfway up the sides of the soufflé dish. Bake until the center of the custard is just set, about 45 minutes. Remove and allow to sit for 15 minutes before serving. Serve warm or at room temperature with warm **Caramel Sauce.**

Serves 8

Caramel Sauce

1 cup heavy cream
1-3/4 cups sugar
3/4 cup water
5 tablespoons cold unsalted butter, cut into pieces
1 teaspoon vanilla extract
1/8 teaspoon salt
2 tablespoons rum, brandy, or bourbon

In a small saucepan over medium heat, warm cream until it almost boils. Cook until scalded or a film forms at the edges. Set aside and keep warm.

Combine sugar and water in a small saucepan over medium heat, then cover and bring to a simmer. Remove lid and increase heat, if needed, to maintain simmer. Do not stir, but scrape down any sugar crystals clinging to side of pan with a pastry brush dipped in water. Watch pan carefully, swirling from time to time, until syrup turns golden brown. Remove from heat and whisk in warm cream in a steady stream. Caramel and cream will bubble dramatically, so stir carefully (wear oven mitts to protect hands). Stir in butter, piece by piece, until completely combined, followed by vanilla, salt, and rum. (*Note:* May be stored indefinitely in refrigerator. Reheat gently to serve.)

Makes 2 cups

OPUS RESTAURANT
Meyerson Symphony Center
Dallas, Texas 75201
(214) 670-3722

Pecan Bread Pudding with Whiskey Sauce

3 large eggs
1-1/4 cups sugar
2 teaspoons vanilla extract
1/2 teaspoon nutmeg
1-1/2 teaspoons cinnamon
1/4 cup melted butter or margarine
2 cups milk
5–6 cups very dry French bread cubes
1/2 cup raisins, dark or golden or combination
1/2 cup toasted pecans

In a large bowl, beat eggs until very frothy with an electric mixer at high speed. Add sugar, vanilla, nutmeg, cinnamon, butter, and milk. Mix very well until sugar is dissolved and mixture becomes smooth.

With a wooden spoon or spatula, stir in bread cubes and mix well, allowing bread to absorb liquid. Fold in raisins and pecans. Pour mixture into a well-greased loaf pan or an 8-by-8-inch square pan. Pour any remaining liquid over bread cubes and set aside to soak for 45 minutes. (This step is very important; don't shortcut the soaking time. Pat down any cubes that float.)

Preheat oven to 300 degrees. Cover pan with foil and bake for 15 to 20 minutes. Remove foil and bake for about 20 minutes more, until pudding is fluffy and well browned. Serve with **Whiskey Sauce.**

Serves 8

Whiskey Sauce

3/4 cup heavy cream
2 tablespoons vanilla extract
1/2 teaspoon cinnamon
1/2 teaspoon nutmeg
2-1/2 teaspoons sugar
3 tablespoons cornstarch dissolved in 3 tablespoons water
1-1/2 tablespoons bourbon

In a small saucepan, combine cream, vanilla, cinnamon, nutmeg, and sugar. Place over medium heat and bring just to a simmer. Using a wire whisk, slowly stir dissolved cornstarch into cream mixture. Simmer for a few minutes more, just until thickened. Remove from heat and stir in bourbon. Serve warm.

Makes about 1 cup

CAMELLIA CAFE
6617 Snider Plaza
Dallas, Texas 75205
(214) 691-8164

Mexican Rice Pudding with Honey and Texas Blueberries

1/2 cup long-grain white rice (not converted rice)
Boiling water
4 cups milk
3/4 cup sugar
Pinch of salt
1 vanilla bean, split lengthwise and scraped, or 1 tablespoon vanilla extract
1/2 teaspoon plus a dash of cinnamon
3 egg yolks
2 teaspoons cornstarch
1 tablespoon unsalted butter, softened
1 teaspoon vanilla extract
3/4 cup heavy cream
1 tablespoon fresh lime juice
2 tablespoons honey
1 pint fresh blueberries

In a small saucepan, top rice with enough boiling water to cover, and cook for 5 minutes; drain well. In a large heavy saucepan, combine rice with 3 cups milk, 1/2 cup sugar, salt, and vanilla bean. Bring to a boil, cover, and reduce heat. Simmer for 45 to 50 minutes or until rice is tender and liquid is absorbed. Transfer pudding to a large bowl and stir in 1/2 teaspoon cinnamon. Set aside.

In a heavy saucepan, combine remaining 1 cup milk and 1/4 cup sugar; bring mixture just to a boil. Remove from heat and allow to cool slightly. In a separate bowl, whisk egg yolks and cornstarch together until well mixed. Add warm milk mixture to egg yolks, whisking constantly. Return milk and eggs to saucepan and return to medium heat. Bring to a boil for 1 minute, whisking constantly, until thickened and smooth.

Force milk and egg mixture through a sieve into the rice, then add softened butter and 1 teaspoon vanilla extract, stirring to mix well. Cover bowl with greased waxed paper and refrigerate overnight. Before serving, beat cream until it holds stiff peaks and gently fold into rice mixture. Whisk lime juice, honey, and dash of cinnamon together in a small bowl until well combined. Toss with blueberries and garnish pudding with berries.

Serves 6

BRAZOS
formerly at
2100 Greenville Avenue
Dallas, Texas

Chocolate Glob

- 3 eggs
- 1-1/2 cups sugar
- 3/4 cup all-purpose flour
- 3/4 cup (1-1/2 sticks) unsalted butter, melted
- 1 cup walnut halves
- 4 ounces high-quality unsweetened baking chocolate, melted
- Whipped cream (optional)

Preheat oven to 350 degrees. Butter an 8-inch square baking dish and set aside.

In a large mixing bowl, beat together eggs, sugar, and flour until fluffy. Slowly blend in melted butter and walnut halves. Pour batter into prepared dish and top with melted chocolate. Swirl chocolate through batter with a knife or spatula until the whole mixture looks rippled.

Bake for 15 to 20 minutes or until the mixture appears cake-like at the edges and gooey (but not "raw") in the center.

Serve warm or at room temperature. Each serving should contain some of the outer cake-like edge and some of the gooey center. Top each piece with whipped cream and serve. (*Note:* Will keep at room temperature for several days. May be reheated to serve.)

Serves 6

PARIGI
3311 Oak Lawn Avenue
Dallas, Texas 75219
(214) 521-0295

White Chocolate Mousse

8 ounces white chocolate
2 cups heavy cream
1/2 cup sugar
2 tablespoons plus 2 teaspoons water
3 egg yolks plus 1 whole egg
1/4 teaspoon vanilla extract
1 teaspoon Kirsch liqueur

Melt chocolate in the top of a double boiler over hot water. Remove from heat and reserve.

Whip cream until stiff peaks form, then refrigerate for later use.

In a small heavy saucepan, combine sugar with water. Place over medium-high heat and boil for 3 to 5 minutes, or until syrupy. Remove from heat.

In a large bowl, combine egg yolks and whole egg, then blend at low speed with an electric mixer for 2 minutes. With mixer running, slowly add syrup. Remove bowl from mixer stand and fold in melted chocolate with a rubber spatula. Next fold in whipped cream, vanilla, and Kirsch. Refrigerate for 4 hours before serving.

Serves 8

CAFE PACIFIC
24 Highland Park Village
Dallas, Texas 75205
(214) 526-1170

Ricotta Almond Flan

1-1/2 cups slivered almonds
1 (15-ounce) carton ricotta cheese
3/4 cup sugar
6 large eggs, beaten
Grated zest of 2 large oranges
1/4 cup dark rum
1 teaspoon vanilla extract
1/2 teaspoon nutmeg

Spread almonds on a baking sheet and bake at 300 degrees until lightly browned, about 10 minutes. Remove from oven and cool. Increase oven temperature to 325 degrees.

Grind almonds fine in a food processor, then blend in ricotta, sugar, eggs, orange zest, rum, vanilla, and nutmeg. Butter a deep pie dish, pour in ricotta mixture, and bake for 30 to 35 minutes or until center of flan is set. Cool before cutting into wedges.

Serves 10

THE MOZZARELLA COMPANY
2944 Elm Street
Dallas, Texas 75226
(214) 741-4072

Fried Apricot Pies

1/3 cup shortening
2 cups self-rising flour
2/3 cup ice water
1 (6-ounce) package dried apricots
1 cup sugar
1/4 teaspoon cinnamon
Vegetable oil for frying
Powdered sugar

Combine shortening and flour in a food processor and pulse several times, until mixture resembles cornmeal. Sprinkle with ice water and pulse again briefly, until dough forms a ball. Remove from work bowl, cover with plastic wrap, and allow to rest for 30 minutes.

Using scissors, snip apricots into 1/2-inch pieces. Place in a heavy saucepan and add enough water to cover. Place a lid on pan and simmer until apricots are tender, then uncover and simmer until almost all liquid has evaporated. Add sugar and cinnamon, stirring over low heat until sugar has dissolved. Remove from heat and cool while dough is resting.

To assemble, divide pastry into 8 round pieces. On a floured board, roll each piece into a 6-inch circle. Place 1/4 cup of filling in the center, moisten edges with a little water, then fold pastry circles in half. Press edges with a fork dipped in flour. (*Note:* At this point, either deep-fry immediately or freeze.)

Preheat oil to 375 degrees. Deep-fry pies for about 3 minutes or until golden brown. (Fry frozen pies at the same temperature, without defrosting, for about 4 minutes.) To prepare in a large skillet, use about 1/2 inch of oil and fry pies over medium-high heat for about 2 minutes per side. Drain on absorbent paper towels, then dust with powdered sugar. Serve warm or at room temperature.

Serves 8

PEGGY SUE BBQ
6600 Snider Plaza
Dallas, Texas 75205
(214) 987-9188

Texas Pecan Pie

1 (9-inch) pie crust, unbaked
1/2 cup heavy cream
3 small eggs, beaten
1 teaspoon vanilla extract
1 cup sugar
1 teaspoon butter, melted
1 cup dark corn syrup
1 cup pecan halves

Preheat oven to 350 degrees. Combine cream, eggs, vanilla, sugar, butter, and corn syrup. Blend at low speed with an electric mixer or by hand until smooth. Stir in pecan halves.

Pour filling into pie crust and bake for 70 minutes, or until filling is set. If crust begins to get too brown, shield it with circle of aluminum foil to just cover edge of crust.

Serves 8

DICK'S LAST RESORT
1701 North Market Street
Dallas, Texas 75202
(214) 747-0001

Black Bottom Pecan Pie

1 ounce bittersweet chocolate
4-1/2 teaspoons heavy cream
1 teaspoon sugar
1 cup plus 2 tablespoons firmly packed light brown sugar
9 tablespoons unsalted butter, melted
5 eggs
1 cup light corn syrup
4-1/2 teaspoons vanilla extract
4-1/2 teaspoons Jack Daniel's bourbon
1 cup chopped pecans

Melt chocolate in the top of a double boiler over simmering, not boiling, water. Remove from heat and reserve.

Heat cream and sugar in a small saucepan over low heat, just until sugar dissolves. Stir in melted chocolate and blend well. Cool completely and spread evenly over bottom of a chilled **Pie Crust.** Place filled crust in freezer to chill.

Preheat oven to 350 degrees. Combine brown sugar and melted butter in a medium bowl. Beat with an electric mixer at medium-low speed until smooth and sugar has dissolved. Add eggs, one at a time, blending well after each addition. Add corn syrup, mixing well, followed by vanilla and bourbon.

Remove **Pie Crust** from freezer and arrange pecans on the bottom. Pour egg mixture over pecans and bake until center of pie is set, about 45 minutes.

Serves 8

Pie Crust

2 cups cake flour
4 tablespoons sugar
1 tablespoon salt
1 cup shortening, chilled
1 tablespoon ice water

Sift together flour, sugar, and salt. Cut in shortening until mixture has texture of cornmeal. Add ice water and mix to form dough. (Add more ice water, a few drops at a time, if necessary to form dough.) Shape into a ball and refrigerate for at least 30 minutes. Roll out on a floured board to 11 inches in diameter. Transfer to a 9-inch pie pan, trim excess around edges, flute, and refrigerate for 1 hour.

BABY ROUTH
2708 Routh Street
Dallas, Texas 75201
(214) 871-2345

Coconut Amaretto Pie

1 (8- or 9-inch) pie crust, unbaked
3 eggs
1-1/2 cups sugar
1/2 cup (1 stick) unsalted butter, melted
1 teaspoon vanilla extract
1 cup sweetened, flaked coconut
6 amaretti cookies, crumbled (about 1/2 cup)

Preheat oven to 400 degrees. Beat eggs lightly and stir in sugar, butter, vanilla, and coconut. Mix well. Pour filling into unbaked pie crust and sprinkle evenly with cookie crumbs.

Bake at 400 degrees for 10 minutes, then lower temperature to 375 degrees and bake for 15 minutes more. Lower temperature again, to 350 degrees, and bake for 15 to 20 minutes or until center of pie is set. Cool completely before slicing.

Serves 8

AMORE
6931 Snider Plaza
Dallas, Texas 75205
(214) 739-0502

Flourless Chocolate Cake

14 egg yolks
2-3/4 cups sugar
10 egg whites
1-1/2 cups cocoa, sifted

Preheat oven to 350 degrees. Grease a 10-inch springform pan and set aside.
In a stainless steel mixing bowl, beat egg yolks and 1-3/4 cups sugar together until light and fluffy. (Mixture should be a pale yellow.) In another stainless steel bowl, beat egg whites until foamy. Gradually add remaining 1 cup sugar and beat until mixture forms stiff peaks.

Gently fold cocoa into yolk mixture. Fold yolk mixture into egg whites until thoroughly combined. Pour batter into prepared pan and bake for about 45 minutes or until cake appears set. Remove from oven and cool on a rack in the pan. (Cake will sink considerably.) When cool, refrigerate for 3 to 4 hours, then release sides of pan and serve.

Serves 10

THE FRENCH ROOM
The Adolphus Hotel
1321 Commerce Street
Dallas, Texas 75202
(214) 742-8200

Pride of Texas Chocolate Cake with Chocolate Frosting

2 cups all-purpose flour
2 cups sugar
1 teaspoon cinnamon
1 teaspoon baking soda
1/4 teaspoon salt
1 cup (2 sticks) butter or margarine
1/3 cup cocoa
1 cup water
1/2 cup buttermilk
2 eggs
1 teaspoon vanilla extract

Preheat oven to 400 degrees. Grease and flour a 10-by-15-inch jelly-roll pan and set aside.

Combine flour, sugar, cinnamon, baking soda, and salt in a large bowl. Mix well, then set aside.

In a small saucepan over high heat, combine butter, cocoa, and water. Bring mixture to a boil, then pour over dry ingredients and mix well. Combine buttermilk, eggs, and vanilla, and add to cocoa mixture. Mix well, then pour into prepared pan. Bake for 20 to 25 minutes or until center springs back when touched.

While cake is baking, prepare **Chocolate Frosting.** Pour warm frosting over warm cake, spreading evenly. Cool in pan, cut into squares, and serve.

Makes 35 (2-inch) squares

Chocolate Frosting

1/2 cup (1 stick) butter or margarine
1/4 cup cocoa
6 tablespoons milk
4 cups powdered sugar
1 cup toasted, chopped pecans

In a small saucepan, combine butter, cocoa, and milk over high heat. Bring mixture to a boil, then pour over sugar in a large bowl. Add nuts and mix well. Keep warm until ready to spread over cake.

Makes 2 cups

CITY MARKET
Trammel Crow Centre
2001 Ross Avenue, Suite 200
Dallas, Texas 75201
(214) 979-2690

Semisweet Chocolate Cake

10 ounces semisweet chocolate
1-1/4 cups (2-1/2 sticks)
 unsalted butter
9 egg yolks
1-1/3 cups sugar
5 egg whites
Pinch of salt
1 teaspoon vanilla extract

Preheat oven to 325 degrees. Line the inside of a 9-inch cake pan with foil, leaving plenty of overlap on the sides for easier handling. Set aside.

Melt chocolate and butter in the top of a double boiler over simmering, not boiling, water. Remove from heat and cool.

In a large bowl, beat egg yolks and sugar for 3 to 4 minutes or until mixture turns pale yellow. In another large bowl, beat egg whites and salt until stiff peaks form.

Fold egg whites into yolk mixture in thirds, along with vanilla. Pour mixture into prepared pan and sit cake pan in a larger pan. Pour enough hot water into the larger pan to come 1 inch up the sides of the cake pan. Place in oven and bake for 20 to 30 minutes, or until top looks fairly dry and feels stiff to the touch. (The inside will be slightly liquid.)

Let cool in the pan, then cover with plastic wrap and refrigerate for 2 hours or until cake remains stiff as foil is lifted out of pan. Invert onto a serving tray and peel away foil. Heat a metal spatula by dipping it in hot water. Quickly dry spatula and run it along sides and top of cake until there is enough melting to resemble an icing. (Reheat and dry spatula as needed.) Slice and serve.

Serves 12 to 14

CITY CAFE
5757 West Lovers Lane
Dallas, Texas 75209
(214) 351-2233

Double Chocolate Cheesecake

1-1/2 cups Oreo cookie crumbs
1/3 cup butter, melted
1-1/2 cups sugar
1/2 cup finely chopped nuts
2 (8-ounce) packages cream cheese, softened
1/3 cup cocoa
1-1/2 teaspoons vanilla extract
2 eggs
1 cup sour cream
Fresh raspberries
Mint leaves

Preheat oven to 300 degrees. In a medium bowl, thoroughly combine cookie crumbs with melted butter, 2 tablespoons sugar, and nuts. Press onto bottom and slightly up sides of a greased 10-inch springform pan. Set aside.

In a large bowl, beat cream cheese and 1-1/4 cups sugar with an electric mixer. When cream cheese is fluffy and all sugar is incorporated, add cocoa and 1 teaspoon vanilla, mixing until well blended. Add eggs and mix again until well blended.

Pour mixture into crust. Wrap bottom and sides of springform pan with a double thickness of aluminum foil and place inside a larger pan. Add enough hot water to large pan to come 1 inch up the sides of springform pan. Transfer to oven and bake for 3 hours, or until cake recedes from sides of pan and the center is firm.

Just before baking time is complete, combine sour cream, remaining 2 tablespoons sugar, and remaining 1/2 teaspoon vanilla. Remove cheesecake from oven and spread sour cream mixture evenly over top. Discard hot water and larger pan; return cheesecake to oven for 5 minutes more. Cool and serve garnished with fresh raspberries and mint leaves.

Serves 10

HUNTINGTON'S
Westin Hotel Galleria Dallas
13340 Dallas Parkway
Dallas, Texas 75240
(214) 851-2882

Kahlúa Brownies

- 1/2 cup (1 stick) butter
- 4 ounces unsweetened chocolate
- 4 eggs, room temperature
- 1/2 teaspoon salt
- 1/4 teaspoon vanilla extract
- 2 teaspoons Kahlúa liqueur
- 2 cups sugar
- 1 cup all-purpose flour
- 2/3 cup chopped walnuts
- 2/3 cup semisweet chocolate chips

Preheat oven to 350 degrees. Grease and flour a 9-by-13-inch baking pan and set aside.

Melt butter and unsweetened chocolate in the top of a double boiler over hot, not boiling, water. Set aside and allow mixture to cool.

Using an electric mixture, beat eggs until light and foamy, then add salt, vanilla, and Kahlúa. Add sugar gradually, beating constantly.

Stir in reserved chocolate mixture by hand, followed by flour, walnuts, and chocolate chips. Pour batter into prepared pan and bake for 25 minutes or until a toothpick inserted comes out clean. Cool completely before cutting and serving.

Makes 24 (2-inch) squares

DRAGON STREET DINER
1444 Oak Lawn Avenue
Dallas, Texas 75207
(214) 747-1566

Warm Minted Sweet Biscuits with Strawberries and White Chocolate Ice Cream

3 cups cake flour
2-1/4 cups sugar
1-1/2 tablespoons baking powder
1 teaspoon salt
3/4 cup vegetable shortening
2 eggs
1/2 cup milk
2 tablespoons chopped fresh mint
1 teaspoon vanilla extract
3-1/2 pints strawberries
2 tablespoons Grand Marnier liqueur
2 cups heavy cream
Powdered sugar
6–8 mint sprigs

In a large bowl, combine flour, 1 cup sugar, baking powder, and salt. Cut shortening into dry ingredients with a fork or electric mixer. Set aside.

In another bowl, beat together eggs and milk, blending until smooth. Add milk mixture and chopped mint to dry ingredients, mixing thoroughly. (Dough should be thinner and stickier than regular shortcake or biscuit dough.) Refrigerate for at least 30 minutes.

Rinse and slice 5 cups strawberries. Puree remaining 2 cups strawberries with 1 cup sugar and Grand Marnier. Pour pureed strawberries over sliced berries and fold together. Set aside.

Whip cream with remaining 1/4 cup sugar until soft peaks form. Refrigerate until ready to serve.

Preheat oven to 350 degrees. Remove chilled dough from refrigerator and place on a well-floured surface. Roll or pat by hand to 3/4-inch thickness. Cut dough with a biscuit cutter into 6 to 8 (4-inch) biscuits and place on a greased baking sheet. Bake biscuits for 12 minutes or until golden brown.

Slice biscuits in half while still hot. Spoon strawberry filling onto bottom halves and then dollop whipped cream onto filling. Dust reserved biscuit tops with powdered sugar, place tops over whipped cream layer, and garnish each with a mint sprig. Serve with **White Chocolate Ice Cream.**

Serves 6 to 8

White Chocolate Ice Cream

3/4 cup milk
10 ounces white chocolate, finely chopped
1/2 teaspoon vanilla extract
2 cups heavy cream, room temperature

Place milk and chocolate in a large bowl and set over a saucepan of barely simmering water. Stir occasionally until chocolate melts. Set aside and cool to room temperature.

Stir vanilla and cream into cooked chocolate mixture and pour through a fine strainer into the canister of an ice cream maker or machine. Freeze according to manufacturer's directions.

Makes about 1 quart

ROUTH STREET CAFE
formerly at
3005 Routh Street
Dallas, Texas

Raisin Scones

4 cups all-purpose flour
2 cups whole wheat flour
1/4 teaspoon salt
3/4 cup sugar
2 tablespoons baking powder
1-1/2 cups raisins
3 eggs
1 tablespoon vanilla extract
1-1/2 cups heavy cream
1 cup melted butter

Preheat oven to 375 degrees. Into a large bowl, sift together flours, salt, sugar, and baking powder. Stir in raisins. In another large bowl, combine eggs, vanilla, and cream, then stir in melted butter. Add dry ingredients and stir until moistened.

Roll or pat dough out on a floured surface to 1-1/2 inches thick. Cut into 10 or 12 (2- to 2-1/2-inch) rounds. Arrange rounds 1 inch apart on an ungreased baking sheet and bake until golden brown, about 15 to 20 minutes.

Serves 6 to 8

DREAM CAFE
The Quadrangle
2800 Routh Street
Dallas, Texas 75201
(214) 954-0486

Sicilian Cannoli

12 ounces mascarpone (Italian cream cheese; see note), softened
1/2 cup chopped pistachio nuts
1/2 cup mini chocolate chips
1/3 cup finely chopped candied fruit
3/4 cup blueberries, rinsed and dried
14 to 18 cannoli shells
Powdered sugar
Mint leaves

Using a spatula, fold nuts, chocolate chips, and candied fruit into mascarpone. Fold in berries last, being careful not to crush.

Fill cannoli shells with mixture and sprinkle shells with powdered sugar. Garnish with fresh mint leaves and serve.

(*Note:* You can make your own mascarpone as follows: In a small saucepan over medium heat, combine 1 cup sugar and 1/4 cup water. Bring to a boil, then reduce to low heat and simmer, stirring frequently, for 10 minutes or until mixture becomes syrupy. Remove from heat and cool completely. Soften 8 ounces of ricotta cheese and 4 ounces of cream cheese at room temperature and then combine in a bowl, using a spatula. Sweeten to taste with cooled sugar syrup.)

Serves 6 to 8

PATRIZIO
25 Highland Park Village
Dallas, Texas 75205
(214) 522-7878

Banana Split Chimichangas

8 ounces bittersweet chocolate, chopped into small pieces
6 tablespoons unsalted butter
1 cup heavy cream
4 (6-inch) flour tortillas
1 ripe banana, peeled and quartered lengthwise
1/2 cup chopped macadamia nuts
1 pint vanilla ice cream
1 egg, beaten
2 to 3 cups vegetable oil
Powdered sugar

Combine chocolate, butter, and cream in the top of a double boiler over simmering, not boiling water. Stir occasionally until all ingredients are melted and well combined. Set aside and allow to cool.

Heat a skillet or griddle over medium-high heat. (Do not grease.) Place tortillas over heat to soften enough to become pliable. Remove from heat and arrange 1 piece of banana, about 1/4 cup cooled chocolate mixture, 2 tablespoons nuts, and 2 tablespoons ice cream off center on each tortilla.

Brush inside edges of tortillas with beaten egg. Fold top edge of tortilla about a quarter of the way over filling. Repeat with bottom edge. Starting with the unfolded edge closest to the filling, roll into a shape like an egg roll. Freeze for several hours or overnight. Keep frozen until ready to serve.

Just before serving, heat oil in a skillet or deep-fryer to 400 degrees. Place tortilla rolls in hot oil until golden brown on all sides, about 3 minutes. Dust with powdered sugar and serve immediately.

Serves 4

LAUREL'S
Sheraton Park Central Hotel
12720 Merit Drive
Dallas, Texas 75251
(214) 851-2021

Taco Sundaes with Fruit Salsa

4 (6-inch) flour tortillas
Vegetable oil for frying
Cinnamon sugar (or substitute 1 teaspoon cinnamon mixed with 1/4 cup sugar)
4 scoops vanilla ice cream
4 tablespoons whipped cream
4 sprigs mint

Heat 1 inch of vegetable oil in a skillet over high heat. When oil is hot, lower heat to medium and fry tortillas one at a time, just until they begin to puff and turn golden.

Remove from hot oil and quickly drape over an inverted bowl with steep sides. Drain, and allow to cool and harden into a bowl shape. When cool, sprinkle inside and out with a liberal dusting of cinnamon sugar. (*Note:* Shells may be made in advance and reserved.)

To serve, fill each shell with a scoop of vanilla ice cream and spoon equal portions of **Fruit Salsa** over each. Garnish with whipped cream and mint sprigs.

Serves 4

Fruit Salsa

1-1/2 cups chopped peaches
1-1/2 cups chopped strawberries
2 tablespoons sugar
1 tablespoon finely chopped crystallized ginger
1/2 teaspoon grated lemon peel

Combine all ingredients in a large bowl and toss gently to blend. Serve at room temperature. (Refrigerate unused portions.)

Makes 3 cups

CAFE VERDE
Southland Center Hotel
400 North Olive Street
Dallas, Texas 75201-4001
(214) 922-0325

Summer Peach Baklava

1 pound phyllo pastry or strudel dough, thawed overnight in refrigerator
5 cups finely chopped walnuts
3 cups sugar
2 tablespoons cinnamon
2 cups (4 sticks) butter
5 fresh peaches, peeled, pitted, and coarsely chopped
1 cup water
6 whole cloves
Grated zest of 1 orange and 1 lemon
1 cup honey

In a large bowl, mix walnuts, 1 cup sugar, and 1 tablespoon cinnamon, and set aside.

Melt 1/2 cup (1 stick) butter in a saucepan over low heat. Add peaches and simmer until mixture is thick, about 25 minutes. As peaches soften, mash with the back of a spoon. Transfer mixture to a shallow pan and chill completely in the refrigerator.

Melt remaining butter. Grease a 10-by-16-by-2-inch pan. Remove phyllo sheets from package and wrap in a damp towel. Working quickly, brush a sheet with butter and place in prepared pan. Repeat with 7 more sheets. Sprinkle half the nut mixture over pastry sheets. Brush 5 more sheets with butter and layer over nut mixture. Spread cooled peach mixture over pastry. Top peaches with another 5 buttered sheets. Spread pastry with remaining nut mixture. Top with 7 more buttered sheets and 1 without butter.

With a small sharp knife, cut pastry into 1-1/2-by-1-1/2-inch diamonds by making diagonal cuts. (Be sure and cut all the way to the bottom.) Using a spray bottle filled with water, spritz top of pastry generously to prevent curling in the oven. Bake in a 325-degree oven for 60 to 90 minutes, until top is golden brown.

Place remaining 2 cups sugar, water, cloves, remaining 1 tablespoon cinnamon, and orange and lemon zest in a small saucepan over medium heat. Boil for 10 minutes, then add honey and allow to cool slightly. Strain syrup and set aside. When baklava comes out of the oven, pour syrup over pastry. Chill overnight before serving.

Serves 12

GALLERY RESTAURANT
Dallas Museum of Art
1717 North Harwood Street
Dallas, Texas 75201
(214) 922-1260

Strawberries with Black Pepper

1 teaspoon whole black peppercorns
2 pints strawberries, cleaned and halved
Sugar to taste
1-1/2 tablespoons brandy
2-1/2 tablespoons Grand Marnier liqueur

Place peppercorns on a cutting board or in a mortar. Using a heavy object, such as the flat side of a knife or a pestle, crack peppercorns. (Do not use a pepper mill; the grind will be too fine.)

Place strawberries in a bowl and sprinkle with sugar to taste. Add brandy, Grand Marnier, and cracked peppercorns. Marinate for 15 minutes, then serve in individual bowls.

Serves 4

CAFE PACIFIC
24 Highland Park Village
Dallas, Texas 75205
(214) 526-1170

White Chocolate–Chocolate Monster Cookies

2 cups (4 sticks) unsalted butter, softened
1-1/3 cups sugar
3/4 cup firmly packed light brown sugar
3-1/3 cups all-purpose flour
2/3 cup dark cocoa
1 teaspoon salt
1 tablespoon vanilla extract
1-2/3 cups roasted pecans, chopped
8 ounces white chocolate, coarsely chopped

Using an electric mixer, beat together butter and sugars until mixture becomes fluffy. Sift together flour, cocoa, and salt, then stir into butter mixture. Beat in vanilla and pecans, mixing well.

Scoop out dough by 1/4-cupfuls (about 3 ounces by weight or the size of a racquetball) and shape into balls around 1 to 2 tablespoons of white chocolate chunks. Chill for 1 or 2 hours on foil-lined baking sheets.

Preheat oven to 350 degrees. Place cookies on ungreased baking sheets and flatten slightly with the palm of your hand. Bake for about 10 minutes or until edges begin to crisp. (Do not overbake; cookies will be slightly gooey in the middle, but will firm as they cool.) Cool on racks and serve.

Makes about 24 cookies

MAIN STREET NEWS
2934 Main Street
Dallas, Texas 75226
(214) 746-2934

Restaurants

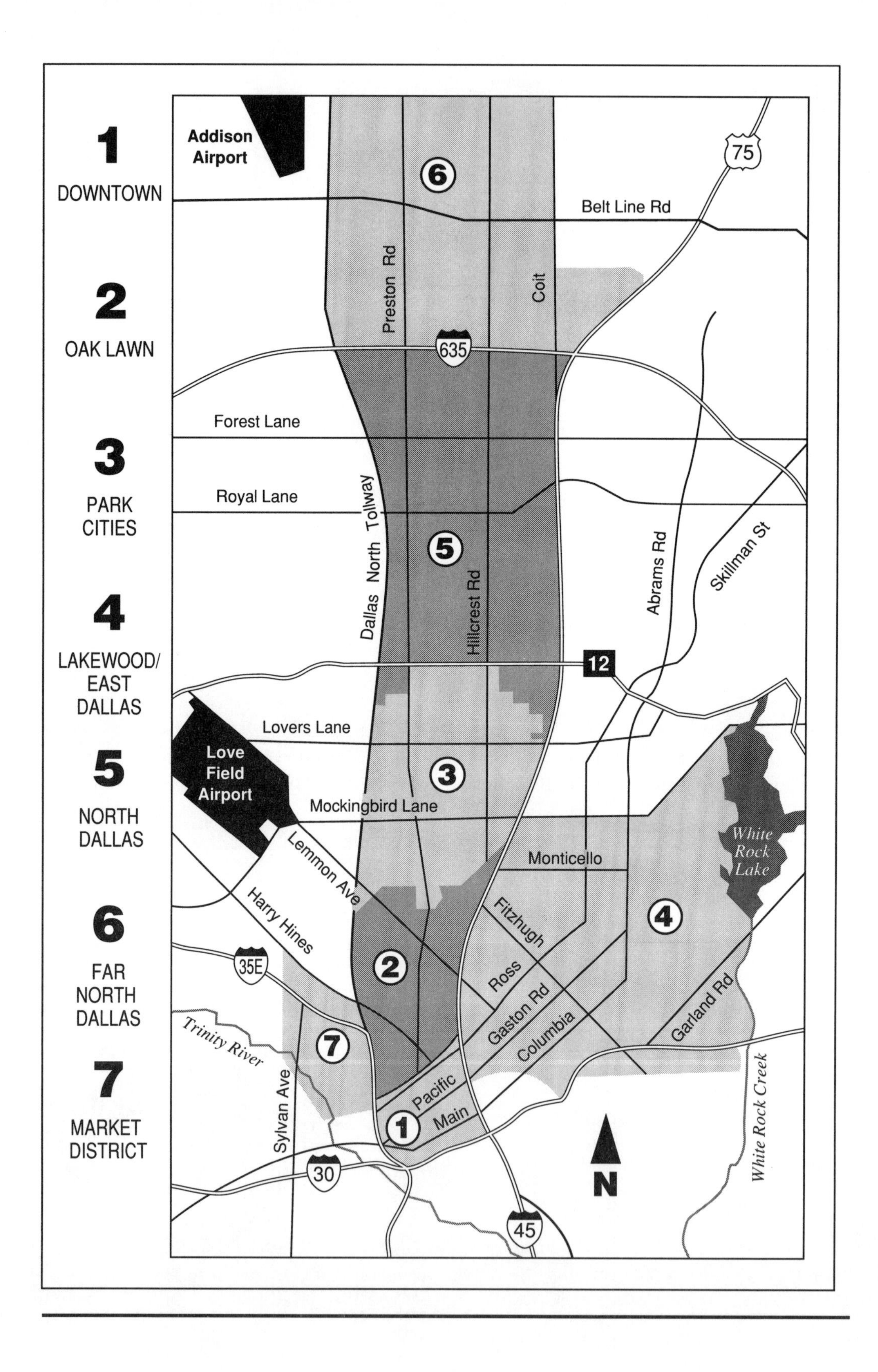

1
DOWNTOWN
2
OAK LAWN
3
PARK CITIES
4
LAKEWOOD/ EAST DALLAS
5
NORTH DALLAS
6
FAR NORTH DALLAS
7
MARKET DISTRICT
Addison Airport
75
Belt Line Rd
Preston Rd
Coit
635
Forest Lane
Royal Lane
Dallas North Tollway
Hillcrest Rd
Abrams Rd
Skillman St
12
Lovers Lane
Love Field Airport
Mockingbird Lane
Monticello
Lemmon Ave
Harry Hines
Fitzhugh
White Rock Lake
35E
Ross
Gaston Rd
Columbia
Garland Rd
Trinity River
Sylvan Ave
Pacific
Main
White Rock Creek
N
30
45

Restaurant Listings

The following listings offer additional information about the restaurants represented in the recipe sections of this book.

KEY:
Prices/credit cards: $ (under $10); $$ ($10 to $20); $$$ ($20 and up); ☐ (credit cards accepted); no ☐ (credit cards not accepted)
Dress: C (casual); D (dressy)
Map locations: (1) Downtown; (2) Oak Lawn; (3) Park Cities; (4) East Dallas/ Lakewood; (5) North Dallas; (6) Far North Dallas/Richardson; (7) Market District

Actuelle, 500 Crescent Ct., Ste. 165, Dallas, TX 75201; (214) 855-0440. This establishment features New American cuisine by renowned chef Victor Gielisse in an elegant, but not stuffy, setting. Polish without pomp. $$$; ☐; D; (1)

Amore, 6931 Snider Plaza, Dallas, TX 75205; (214) 739-0502. This family-casual place is very popular, with a devoted following for its excellent Italian cuisine. The homemade desserts are addictive. $$; ☐; C; (3)

August Moon, 15030 Preston Rd., Dallas TX 75240 (214) 385-7227; 2300 N. Central Expwy., Plano, TX 75074 (214) 881-0071. These beautifully decorated spots offer unusual Chinese dishes. There's a popular buffet at the Plano location. Favorite dishes include whole red snapper, Hunan-style. $$; ☐; C; (5)

Baby Routh, 2708 Routh St., Dallas, TX 75201; (214) 871-2345. Here you'll find New American/Southwestern cuisine by up-and-coming chef Kevin Rathbun, whose eclectic touch with ethnic ingredients can be fascinating. A hip place to be seen. $$$; ☐; C; (2)

Beau Nash, Hotel Crescent Court, 400 Crescent Ct., Dallas, TX 75201; (214) 871-3240. This American brasserie houses a legendary bar and fixes great pizzas for snacking. A prime place for people-watching. $$; ☐; C; (1)

Belvedere, Crest Park Hotel, 4242 Lomo Alto, Dallas, TX 75219; (214) 528-6510. This cozy, romantic, Austrian-Swiss restaurant specializes in venison and veal dishes. $$$; ☐; D; (3)

Blue Mesa Grill, 5100 Beltline Rd., Ste. 500, Dallas, TX 75240; (214) 934-0165. Duck taquitos, blue corn enchiladas, and adobe pie are just some of the contemporary Southwestern offerings featured in this folksy Santa Fe setting. $; ☐; C; (6)

Bluebonnet Cafe, Whole Foods Market, 2218 Greenville Ave., Dallas, TX 75206; (214) 824-1744. Delicious natural and vegetarian dishes are served with style in this '60s-inspired natural foods supermarket. A popular spot for breakfast. $; ☐; C; (4)

Brazos. (*Editor's note:* Although Nancy Beckham's wonderful restaurant has now closed, we are pleased to offer readers a sampling here of her truly Texan recipes.)

Cafe Pacific, 24 Highland Park Village, Dallas, TX 75205; (214) 526-1170. Elegant European ambience, with polished marble floors, paneled walls, and crisp white linens, creates a memorable setting for excellent seafood. $$$; ☐; D; (3)

Cafe Verde, Southland Center Hotel, 400 N. Olive St., Dallas, TX 75201-4001; (214) 922-0325. This downtown cafe presents original Southwestern cuisine in a warm friendly atmosphere. The Texas black bean soup and Santa Fe pizza are stand-outs. $$; ☐; C; (1)

Camellia Cafe, 6617 Snider Plaza, Dallas, TX 75205; (214) 691-8164. Cajun and Creole cuisines reign in this family spot near Southern Methodist University. It's fast food–style service, but the meals are superior. $; ☐; C; (3)

Capriccio, 2515 McKinney Ave., Ste. 125, Dallas, TX 75201; (214) 871-2004. Northern Italian cuisine is showcased here in a cozy but elegant Old World setting. Chef and owner Jean Rubede is an excellent host, and the veal chop is a favorite. $$; ☐; C; (2)

Chaplin's, 1928 Greenville Ave., Dallas, TX 75206; (214) 823-3300. Wood-grilled seafood and chops are served in this intimate setting. The salads and seafood tamale appetizer are popular selections. $$; ☐; C; (4)

Chiquita Mexican Cuisine, 4514 Travis St., Ste. 105, Dallas, TX 75205; (214) 521-0092. This place offers genuine Tex-Mex food, plus some seafood specialties as well, in a fun, festive atmosphere. $; ☐; C; (3)

Cisco Grill, 6630 Snider Plaza, Dallas, TX 75205; (214) 363-9506. Tex-Mex, Santa Fe, and Texas-style accents enhance the food at this slick, casual spot. Good burgers, too. $; ☐; C; (3)

City Cafe, 5757 W. Lovers Ln., Dallas, TX 75209; (214) 351-2233. There's popular, casual-chic dining here, along with a superior wine list. This is regional American fare served with style. $$; ☐; C; (3)

City Market, Trammel Crow Centre, 2001 Ross Ave., Ste. 200, Dallas, TX 75201; (214) 979-2690. Gourmet salads, deli sandwiches, and homemade desserts are served up here near downtown in the arts district. $; ☐; C; (1)

Clark's Outpost Bar-B-Q Restaurant, State Hwy. 377, Tioga, TX 76271 (817) 437-2414. The beef and smoked trout here are legendary. And try the calf fries, if you dare. Trust me—this is where Dallas chefs eat barbecue. $; ☐; C; (6)

The Conservatory in the Beau Nash, Hotel Crescent Court, 400 Crescent Ct., Dallas, TX 75201; (214) 871-3242. Cutting-edge seafood is highlighted in this elegant and formal setting. Very romantic, too. $$$; ☐; D; (1)

Dakota's, 600 N. Akard St., Dallas, TX 75201; (214) 740-4001. This New American grill serves meats, seafood, poultry, and game in a stylishly relaxed and elegant setting. There's polished mahogany, brass, and beveled glass galore. $$; ☐; D; (1)

Deep Ellum Cafe, 2706 Elm St., Dallas, TX 75226; (214) 741-9012. The arty crowd and hip staff fit right into this avant garde spot in Dallas's art and entertainment district. Check out the updated versions of comfort food. $$; ☐; C; (4)

Dick's Last Resort, 1701 N. Market St., Dallas, TX 75202; (214) 747-0001. Take your sense of humor to this joint. Sup on wings and ribs, and sip on a wide selection of beers. It's basic bar food except on Sunday, when the gospel brunch is celestial. $$; ☐; C; (1)

Dragon Street Diner, 1444 Oak Lawn Ave., Dallas, TX 75207; (214) 747-1566. Here's cafeteria-style service in a gray, black, and white contemporary setting. Lunch specials include fresh salads, pasta dishes, and wonderful sandwiches. $; ☐; C; (7)

Dream Cafe, The Quadrangle, 2800 Routh St., Dallas, TX 75201; (214) 954-0486. This cafe's version of natural and vegetarian cuisine is perfect for people who don't like "health food." A great breakfast spot. $; ☐; C; (2)

Ewald's Continental Restaurant, Stoneleigh Hotel, 2927 Maple Ave., Dallas, TX 75201; (214) 871-2523. A classic continental restaurant with romantic Old World charm, Ewald's is famous for wonderful steaks and a snapper prepared with white wine and mushrooms. $$$; ☐; D; (2)

Franki's Li'l Europe, 362 Casa Linda Plaza, Dallas, TX 75218; (214) 320-0426. This neighborhood restaurant serves home-style European dishes—Hungarian, Slovenian, and German—in a casual, friendly atmosphere. $$; ☐; C; (4)

The French Room, The Adolphus Hotel, 1321 Commerce St., Dallas, TX 75202; (214) 742-8200. Chef Kevin Garvin has updated this room and calls the cuisine "neoclassic"—contemporary interpretations of French classics. $$$; ☐; D; (1)

Gallery Restaurant, Dallas Museum of Art, 1717 N. Harwood St., Dallas, TX 75201; (214) 922-1260. Ethnic-flavored contemporary American dishes, plus soups and salads, are the specialties here. An artistic oasis at the edge of downtown's concrete corridors. $; □; C; (1)

Gaspar's, 150 S. Denton Tap Rd., Coppell, TX 75019 (214) 393-5152. This European-inspired bistro near DFW airport has a menu that changes every two months and features Swiss, German, Italian, French, and Alpine cuisine. $$$; □; C; (6)

Good Eats Restaurant, Corporate Offices, 3888 Oak Lawn Ave., Dallas, TX 75219; (214) 522-0570 (4 locations). Home-cooking, mesquite grill, and a top-notch chicken-fried steak are served here in an upbeat, homey atmosphere. $; □; C; (2)

The Grape Restaurant, 2808 Greenville Ave., Dallas, TX 75206; (214) 828-1981. The mushroom soup is a must at this intimate bistro with an excellent wine bar attached. $$; □; C; (4)

Hard Rock Cafe, 2601 McKinney Ave., Dallas, TX 75204; (214) 855-0007. Rock memorabilia and a darn good barbecue pork sandwich standout at this noisy, high-energy place. $$; □; C; (2)

Huntington's, The Westin Hotel Galleria Dallas, 13340 Dallas Pkwy., Dallas, TX 75240 (214) 851-2882. New American cuisine is served here in the splendor of an English drawing room. Dishes using ostrich, a low-fat, low-cholesterol beef substitute, are popular selections, as are others on the totally Texas menu. $$; □; D; (6)

Lady Primrose's Thatched Cottage Pantry, The Crescent, 2200 Cedar Springs Rd., Dallas, TX 75201; (214) 871-8334. This store is so full of English antiques, you can hardly tear yourself away to find the tea room. Sample the light sandwiches and country tea pastries. $; □; C; (1)

Landmark Restaurant, Omni Melrose Hotel, 3015 Oak Lawn Ave., Dallas, TX 75219; (214) 521-5151. Innovative New American cuisine with strong Southwestern and Asian accents is created here by rising-star chef Kent Rathbun. $$$; □; D; (2)

Laurel's, Sheraton Park Central Hotel, 12720 Merit Dr., Dallas, TX 75251; (214) 851-2021. This lovely dining room affords guests one of the best views of the city. Wild game specialties are artfully done. $$$; □; D; (5)

Le Caviste. (*Editor's note*: Although this casually elegant restaurant has closed its doors, we are delighted to present a memento of the former house specialties.)

Main Street News, 2934 Main St., Dallas, TX 75226; (214) 746-2934. This European-style bistro serves specialty coffees along with international newspapers and magazines for leisurely reading. $$; ☐; C; (4)

The Mansion on Turtle Creek, 2821 Turtle Creek Blvd., Dallas, TX 75219; (214) 559-2100. Southwest superstar chef Dean Fearing cooks up lobster tacos and authentic tortilla soup here in one of the city's best dining rooms. The clientele is star-studded, too. $$$; ☐; D; (2)

Massimo da Milano, 5519 W. Lovers Ln., Dallas, TX 75209; (214) 351- 1426 (4 other locations). This Italian bakery presents excellent salads and pizzas along with breads, cookies, and pastries. $$; ☐; C; (3)

Mi Piaci, 14854 Montfort, Dallas, TX 75240; (214) 934-8424. Authentic Northern Italian food is featured in a beautiful setting, replete with wood-burning ovens and contemporary Italian decor. $$; ☐; C; (6)

Mia's Tex-Mex Restaurant, 4322 Lemmon Ave., Dallas, TX 75219; (214) 526-1020. Famous for fajitas and homemade chiles rellenos, this neighborhood spot is a mom-and-pop Dallas dining institution. $; ☐; C; (2)

The Mozzarella Company, 2944 Elm St., Dallas, TX 75226; (214) 741-4072. This cheese factory and store offers take-out only, but it's worth the trip if you love fresh mozzarella, mascarpone, and ricotta. The cheeses are available by mail order, too. $; ☐; C; (4)

Nana Grill, Loews Anatole Hotel, 2201 Stemmons Frwy., Dallas, TX 75207; (214) 748-1200. Diners take in a beautiful view of downtown from this high-rise spot, where chef Ron Rosenbaum produces tasty fare in a comfortable setting. $$; ☐; D; (8)

Nero's Italian, 2104 Greenville Ave., Dallas, TX 75206; (214) 826-6376. This small, crowded restaurant executes a rich Italian menu in a dark, romantic setting. $$; ☐; C; (4)

Opus Restaurant, Meyerson Symphony Center, Dallas, TX 75201; (214) 670-3722. On performance nights only, diners can enjoy New American cuisine in the wings of the striking architectural masterpiece housing the Dallas Symphony Orchestra. $$; ☐; D; (1)

Parigi, 3311 Oak Lawn Ave., Dallas, TX 75219; (214) 521-0295. Californian and Italian accents add interest to the New American cuisine created in this casual, chic spot, where it seems you always run into someone you know. $$$; ☐; C; (2)

Patrizio, 25 Highland Park Village, Dallas, TX 75205; (214) 522-7878. Guests find an appealing combination here—good value and an authentic Italian food hall setting that's decorated with 18th-century art. An extensive wine list rounds out the offerings. $$; □; C; (3)

Peggy Sue BBQ, 6600 Snider Plaza, Dallas, TX 75205; (214) 987-9188. There's '50s memorabilia on the walls and good barbecue on the grill, but the vegetables, fresh and lightly done, are the show-stoppers here. $; □; C; (3)

Ristorante Savino, 2929 N. Henderson, Dallas, TX 75206; (214) 826-7804. This romantic, casual Italian restaurant specializes in veal Marsala, veal piccata, and seafood pasta. $$; □; C; (4)

Routh Street Cafe. (*Editor's note:* Although Stephan Pyles's restaurant has now closed, his cuisine left an indelible mark on Dallas. We are pleased to offer readers a "taste" of his talents.)

S&D Oyster Company, 2701 McKinney Ave., Dallas, TX 75204; (214) 880-0111. This New Orleans–style establishment provides a bright, cheerful setting, including a "raw bar," and plenty of fried shrimp, po'boys, and broiled fish. $$; □; C; (2)

Uncle Tai's Hunan Yuan, 13350 Dallas Pkwy., Ste. 3370, Dallas, TX 75240; (214) 934-9998. Hot and spicy Hunan-style cooking delights discriminating guests in this understated, elegant setting. $$; □; C; (6)

Watel's, 1923 McKinney Ave., Dallas, TX 75201; (214) 720-0323. Classic French fare is prepared here in a close, romantic atmosphere. Enjoy alfresco dining in the shadow of downtown. $$; □; C; (1)

Restaurant Index

Recipe Index

The bold asterisk (*) preceding a recipe title indicates a "recipe within a recipe"; that is, one that appears within the preparation instructions for a primary recipe, but which in some cases could stand alone or be served with another favorite dish.

BEGINNINGS

MAIN COURSES

SWEET ENDINGS

About the Author

Dotty Griffith is an award-winning food writer and editor who brings more than 10 years of journalism experience to the task of creating *Dallas Cuisine.* The food editor of the *Dallas Morning News,* she is uniquely qualified to lead hungry readers inside the culinary high spots and interesting eateries of this Texas-sized metropolitan area.

In addition to her newspaper work, Dotty has authored such tasty tomes as *Gourmet Beans, Grains & Rices, Wild About Chili,* and *Wild About Munchies,* and she edited *The Mansion on Turtle Creek Cookbook.*

Dotty also has served as a judge for several national cooking contests and currently co-hosts a daily radio food show.

Order Form

ORDER DIRECT—CALL (800) 877-3119 OR FAX (816) 531-6113

Please rush the following book(s) to me:

____ copy(s) **DALLAS CUISINE** for $14.95 plus $2 shipping
____ copy(s) **SAN DIEGO CUISINE** for $12.95 plus $2 shipping
____ copy(s) **NASHVILLE CUISINE** for $12.95 plus $2 shipping
____ copy(s) **MEMPHIS CUISINE** for $12.95 plus $2 shipping
____ copy(s) **KANSAS CITY CUISINE** for $12.95 plus $2 shipping
____ copy(s) **BRANSON COOKIN' COUNTRY** for $9.95 plus $2 shipping
____ copy(s) **KANSAS CITY GUIDE** for $7.95 plus $2 shipping
____ copy(s) **DAY TRIPS FROM KANSAS CITY** for $8.95 plus $2 shipping
____ copy(s) **DAY TRIPS FROM SAN ANTONIO AND AUSTIN** for $8.95 plus $2 shipping
____ copy(s) **SAN ANTONIO CUISINE** (available summer 1994)

METHOD OF PAYMENT

____ Enclosed is my check for $________ (payable to Two Lane Press, Inc.)
____ Please charge to my credit card: ____ VISA ____ MasterCard
Acct. # ________________________________
Signature ________________________________

SHIP TO: ________________________ **GIFT/SHIP TO:** ________________________
________________________ ________________________
________________________ ________________________
________________________ ________________________
________________________ **FROM:** ________________________

MAIL COMPLETED ORDER FORM TO:
Two Lane Press, Inc. * 4245 Walnut St. * Kansas City, MO 64111